INVESTING FOR BEGINNERS
WHEN THE MISTAKE IS YOU

Matthew McNeill

"If the investor is not experienced, any of his investments will be risky. So what is risky is not the investment but the investor."

-Robert Kiyosaki

Table of Contents

PART II

PART I

PART I

Introduction

This book was compiled to analyze individual investor behavior. Therefore, it was chosen to analyze the main behavioral errors most prevalent among individuals such as heuristics, cognitive and emotional errors, and preference errors.

The first chapter develops from various definitions of what is now considered behavioral finance, for a complete and comprehensive understanding of how this theory has evolved and created a gap with the previous conception of classical financial theory. Subsequently, this chapter will outline and elaborate on the main behavioral difficulties found among individuals, using literature and some examples to intuit how individuals experience impaired reasoning and act irrationally. It will then discuss availability heuristics, representativeness, and anchoring and how these act as mental shortcuts in the decision-making process by generating cognitive and emotional errors such as overconfidence, optimism, regret, and hindsight but also preference errors.

All the errors discussed are derived from studies and research that led to the formulation of a descriptive theory, which will be the focus of the second chapter. Here the prospect theory of Kahneman and Tversky will be expounded, as well as the stages into which the choice process is divided and the value and weighting functions that enable value to be obtained at the valuation stage. In addition, the phenomenon of loss aversion and mental accounting directly attributable to the framing effect, i.e., the critical aspect that emerges from prospect theory, will be explained. It will also discuss its cumulative version and then conclude with a motivational approach.

After analyzing the behavior of the individual investor and what influences his or her decisions, it was decided to introduce the topic of asset management, an excellent way to lead the saver to achieve his or her goals and minimize portfolio risk. Chapter three will then discuss the types of entities that undertake this activity, namely asset management companies. In addition, the concept of a benchmark, as well as a yardstick for defining the risk level of investment, will be discussed. To better understand how an individual can invest his or her savings, we wanted to outline the essentials of the financial field, especially the main instruments of asset management such as funds, investment trusts, asset management, and Exchange Trade Funds. To conclude the chapter, we wanted to focus attention on the individual investor, who, as explored in depth, enacts a range of financial behaviors and choices within the economic environment. In particular, we are going to describe how many investors are inclined to save and how this is managed.

The paper then ends with an empirical study that supports the theoretical discussion given in the previous chapters. The fourth and final chapter presents an analysis carried out on a sample of 79 subjects to show empirical evidence regarding behavioral errors involving individuals. First, a questionnaire was drafted using questions that would prove suitable to highlight and go to verify the most frequent behaviors among the subjects using questions already validated in other studies and questions developed personally. The questionnaire was administered through the web to be able to reach a larger number of people and to enable quick and uncomplicated questionnaire completion.

The results were then processed, and it was possible to divide the analysis process into two stages: an initial descriptive analysis where the characteristics of the target sample will be illustrated through a set of variables such as gender, age, education level, employment status, risk appetite, and economic-financial knowledge. Considerations will be made here that will be useful later in the study of responses related to more specific questions about subjects' behavior.

The other stage of the analysis process is, precisely, the detection of behavioral errors. A study was carried out using the resolutions to the questions posed within the questionnaire, and after all the data were collected, they were analyzed by checking for relevance to the reference theories, enunciated in the previous chapters.

It was intended to bring to life work that is only set out in the first three chapters on a theoretical level but is useful in understanding how the literature can be verified even though limited sample of subjects and what errors are most prevalent among them.

Chapter 1
Behavioral Finance

This paper provides an overview of what are the issues in behavioral finance. In the mid-1970s, this discipline, which challenges the conditions of perfect rationality, began to emerge. It is through the study of an information processing activity that empirical research has demonstrated the limitations of traditional finance in describing the financial decision-making process.

This branch of finance combines aspects involving the field of cognitive psychology with financial theories. It is defined as a descriptive theory that analyzes the behaviors of subjects faced with economic-financial decisions. Behavioral finance thus attempts to explain the way investors reason and the degree to which emotions influence their decisions making, that is, it highlights anomalies in financial markets by analyzing finance and investment from the perspective of individuals' irrationality (Ricciardi and Simon, 2002).

First, the main heuristics, a kind of "shortcut" that is put in place quite unconsciously, will be discussed. Our brain needs some approximations to reduce the complexity of problems and thus limit the effort our memory would have to undergo to store and process a large amount of information. In this chapter, I will talk about availability, representativeness, and anchoring heuristics as they have the function of filtering and selecting information that appears complex in our minds so as to speed up the decision time.

In finance, however, they can lead to inappropriate choices by generating systematic errors that negatively impact the process. Jones (1999) pointed out how decision-makers fail in important decisions because of human cognitive and emotional architecture. The predisposition to err is referred to in technical jargon as bias, literally "prejudice," which is something that precedes judgment and arises as a consequence of heuristics. I will illustrate the main cognitive and emotional errors such as overconfidence, optimism, regret, and hindsight.

Moreover, having evolved into a system in which we seek to deviate from the standards of absolute rationality, we are exposed to an innumerable amount of preference errors, i.e., violations of rationality processes attributable to effects analyzed especially in the conclusion of the chapter. In this regard, I consider it appropriate to mention the

theory in which Miller (1956) verified that individuals can memorize as many as seven items in the same instant, with a variation of plus or minus two depending on individual characteristics. A person does not have such a broad mental capacity to optimize all the variables available to him, so financial decision-making is partly the result of rational thoughts, but it is also influenced by the context of interaction.

1.1 Rationality of perceptions

Individuals make mistakes at both the information gathering and information processing stages because they are conditioned by stereotypes, references, or familiar situations. At the stage when investors gather information, they are influenced by the ease with which they can recall it; in processing, on the other hand, investors judge the likelihood of an event by how representative it appears to be of a set of events regardless of its frequency; they also anchor their thinking to a situation they consider considerable.

Heuristics are thus a set of processes and techniques that enable people to solve complex problems with little available information. The main types were identified by Kahneman and Tversky in 1974 and will be analyzed below.

1.1.1 Availability heuristics

Kahneman and Tversky (1974) give a clear definition of availability heuristics by arguing that there are several situations in which people evaluate the frequency of a class or the likelihood of an event occurring based on how easy that instance is to recall.

Individuals in fact judge events to be easier to remember, and a variety of research shows that it is easier to bring to mind numerous rather than rare events.

In support of this phenomenon, several studies have indeed been carried out, in 1999 Shefrin proposed to a group of people a question where he asked which was the main cause of death in the United States between heart attack and homicide. Most answered homicide because they were influenced by the media which caused them to overlook the fact that heart attack cases were higher. The same is true for financial markets, research conducted shows how the trend of the market is influenced by more recent trends the availability heuristic generates irrational investment choices. In addition to frequency, availability is also influenced by other factors and operates by construction and recovery.

Readiness by construction acts in cases where an event is not easily found in memory, going to create scenarios that make representation easier.

The situation that is going to be constructed will vary and will be influenced by the structure and mental abilities of the subjects, generating an imbalance that could lead to procedural errors.

Rigoni explains how construction goes through imagining a situation, an example being the probability of success attributed to a business plan, which depends on the ease with which strengths and weaknesses are representable. Those that can be imagined with greater intensity could lead to estimation errors.

In addition, there is the availability for retrieval that generates illusory correlation since familiar situations are more easily recalled to mind, but may create false connections between two independent events. Again Rigoni (2006) in this regard exemplifies the concept by describing the situation in which an analyst in assessing the probability of default of a company with dissimilarities is more conditioned by the memory of those companies that have failed by finding themselves in a similar situation, rather than by those cases of companies that have managed to overcome the unstable situation; therefore, more recent events condition the information gathering process more.

Beneath this heuristic is highly persuasive psychological mechanisms that lead subjects to perceptual errors, associations by similarity, and memory selectivity.

1.1.2 Heuristics of representativeness

Representativeness heuristics establish that individuals rely on familiar situations and stereotypes to process information; they then make probability judgments by reasoning from analogies. They also rely on the degree of similarity to the population from which it is drawn and the extent to which it reflects the essential characteristics of the process that generated it. Importantly, this approach, by not taking into account other factors affecting the decision, leads to errors.

One of the errors arising from this heuristic is the tendency to ignore objective frequencies. Although subjects are aware of the probability, they seem to disregard it, contrary to Bayes' theorem.

People are conditioned by superficial information and perform categorizations; an example may take place when there are three people, two of them do not like children while the third one does. If we were asked which one of them is in the teaching profession, using the heuristics of representativeness the decision-maker would opt for the person who likes children. This occurs because in our minds we associate a profession with individuals based on their characteristics, using stereotypes.

Another fallacy is the so-called gambler fallacy, or the tendency to consider small samples to represent a phenomenon. For example, in gambling games, individuals believe that the probability of a random event is greater if it has not occurred for a certain period.

The third error stems from the tendency to assume that extreme assumptions should be matched by extreme consequences; empirical evidence in financial markets shows how forecasts of equities tend to be optimistic or conversely pessimistic based on their performance relative to the market index over a given period.

Finally, the conjunction fallacy, which is the tendency to overestimate the probability of two joint events while downplaying the probability of two disjoint events. Let us compare the probability that the following two situations may occur:

❖ Recession in the U.S. economy

❖ Increase in interest rates that would lead to a change in real estate prices, causing a decrease in consumption and thus a recession of the U.S. economy

Subjects consider the second scenario more likely because it includes more detail and provides a specific explanation of why the U.S. economy might experience a recession. A recession can occur for any reason other than those argued in the second situation, in addition, probability theory explains that the greater the number of details present, the lower the probability of this event occurring. The choice is contingent on whether we can create a more representative picture by having a large number of particularities.

1.1.3 Heuristics of anchoring

The anchoring heuristic like the representativeness heuristic is part of information processing. It states that in the situation where individuals have to make numerical estimates, they tend to anchor themselves to an initial value that may coincide with a previously made estimate, and then change it in the direction they think is correct. This happens because the moment we are asked to give an exact numerical figure about an issue we do not know precisely, we prefer to use any figure as a starting point for the estimate. Kahneman and Tversky (1974) first proved that subjects use these anchors even in cases where: they are informed that the choice of numbers is completely random, the anchors are unlikely digits therefore too low or too high, or that no anchors are present but are mentally created (self-generated anchors).

Anchor heuristics are affected by the tendency of individuals to confirm initial assumptions, and this can be demonstrated with a simple example. Individuals are interviewed and asked to estimate how many African countries are part of the United Nations, and each subject is given a number between 0 and 100 that is completely random. Initially, they were asked whether the assigned number was greater or less than the actual number and immediately afterward to estimate a percentage of countries (Kahneman and Tversky, 1974). When respondents have to answer the second question they are conditioned by the figure given in the previous question so they will try to verify the veracity of the starting conditions. The more they reason, the more they tend to anchor to the initial hypothesis, as a result, the final result does not deviate much from the initial reference point. People believe that the anchor is the right answer, so they try to find as much information to confirm the anchor as possible rather than information that falsifies it; however, if the anchor is not provided, so no number can perform that function, then it will be self-generated and modified by excess or defect depending on what is believed to be the correct answer.

1.2 Cognitive and emotional errors

Analyzing the three main heuristic behaviors reveals how they can generate errors in decision making. While they can facilitate the management of information, they also lead to the creation of overly simple or incorrect solutions. The evaluation bias to which we are subjected generates real systematic errors that are called bias, an expression commonly associated with error even though the literal meaning is "prejudice."

Individuals are predisposed to make cognitive and/or emotional errors leading to a general lack of efficiency in the market and errors in individual investment choices. Studies carried out by Kahneman and Tversky, followed by others, seek to explain such anomalies and exploit them to achieve more productive investment strategies. In the following paragraphs, in particular, we will focus attention on some of the errors that produce judgments contrary to the rationality hypothesis such as overconfidence, optimism, regret, and hindsight.

1.2.1 Excessive security

One of the most frequent biases in investment choices is over-confidence-that is extreme estimation of oneself and one's abilities. This increases presumption and confidence in one's abilities to predict the course of an event. It tends to be the case that the overconfident investor does not realize that he has little information at his disposal and has recently entered the market as opposed to those who have already developed a more objective method of evaluation. More concretely he makes forecasts that are skewed to his advantage and not entirely rational contrary to classical financial theory, which holds that individuals should acquire information until marginal costs equal incremental expected benefit i.e. more information equals better returns.

Investors tend to trade in markets by reducing their expected utility, in the certainty of their beliefs they do not consider additional information and therefore consider their buying and selling choices to be less risky than they are (Barber and Odean, 1999).

In fact, according to scholars, in the case of a loss, the blame falls on an external cause; on the contrary in the case of a gain, investors take credit for it so it increases self-confidence more than it decreases subsequently to negative feedback. In everyday life, this happens when subjects consider themselves aware of how government bonds work, but if they are then asked what relationship there is between price and yield only 11% can answer as well as only 23% can give an explanation to the expression negative yield.

[13]

1.2.2 Optimism

Among the many aspects of overconfidence emerges that of over-optimism, which leads people to dwell solely on the positive aspects of a set of historical data or characteristics of a product. This bias is defined as the difference between what subjects expect and what occurs; if expectations are higher than reality then there is a cognitive bias. If there is no alignment between the event that is thought to happen and what happens, negative consequences are generated due to the absence of precautionary measures. For example, applying sunscreen to avoid skin problems or preserving the respiratory system by avoiding smoking (Weinstein & Klein, 1996).

Individuals overestimate the likelihood of positive outcomes and conversely underestimate negative ones, but this in the financial and business spheres could lead to huge misjudgments.

Excessive optimism can affect entrepreneurial activity, particularly if newly established, as it can lead to protracted unsuccessful business projects negatively impacting not only oneself but also businesses operating in the same field.

Studies conducted by Puri and Robinson (2006), concerning this issue, show that moderately confident individuals, as opposed to those who hold an excessive level of optimism, are less likely to take risks. Moreover, these individuals have a longer planning time horizon, so they save more. About stock investments, they are less likely to engage in speculative activities; conversely, those who demonstrate extreme optimism engage in stock buying and selling activities because they may believe that their stock has a higher return than would be appropriate to believe in correlation with the risk of the stock. Only a moderate dose of optimism should be considered positive for both individual companies and the economy as a whole.

1.2.3 Regret

This type of bias is part of emotional errors so it focuses more on the emotions of individuals when they process and interpret information.

Regret is one of the most important emotional biases and can be generated by dissatisfaction that envelops individuals as they regret not having made a particular decision, or regret not having made a choice that would have been appropriate to implement. Regret, however, can also represent a decision-making bias: before making the choice, the anticipation of regret comes into play, which can lead to immobility and thus to a situation in which the individual is unable to choose; after the decision, on the other hand, individuals may engage in a series of irrational behaviors to contain their dissatisfaction.

They are prone to engage in such behaviors when they are trying to quell the conflict that characterizes them, upon realizing that one of their ideas has turned out to be inaccurate. Fear of regret plays a key role in the process of buying and selling equities, as trying to avoid it can lead to holding losing stocks too long in the portfolio and conversely selling winning stocks too quickly. The explanation lies in the fact that when stocks gain value, to avoid potential regret, they are sold immediately before they experience depreciation. Conversely, losing stocks are sold more reluctantly because selling would mean giving life to the mistake, and the fear of regret is postponed.

Generally, therefore, investor behavior is affected by previous decisions; in particular, those who make substantial gains are more willing to take risks because a paltry gain causes less sorrow than a loss of an equal amount, this is because any negative results will be associated with a reduction in the previous profit. This is referred to as the house money effect and refers to the casino environment in which a player prefers to risk his or her newly won money because it will seem to him or her that he or she is playing not with his or her own money but with the banker's money.

I conclude by pointing out how this error results in the tendency to remain, prisoners of certain decisions because the usefulness of our choices comes from a comparison between the results we obtained and those we could have obtained with different choices.

1.2.4 Hindsight.

Hindsight refers to the tendency of individuals to overestimate the possibility of predicting that a given event will have occurred. Everyone has at least once had the occasion to say "I knew it would happen this way!" in this case, it proved such a mistake.

In finance, especially concerning stock market trends, it is believed that some events such as rises or falls, could be predicted but are determined by random factors.

In 1975 empirical evidence of this error was first demonstrated by Fischhoff and Beyth, who surveyed a group of students before President Nixon visited China and Russia in 1972. Respondents were asked to apply a probability to fifteen questions such as "Will the United States grant China diplomatic recognition?"

When Nixon's trip was over, Fischhoff and Beyth asked the volunteers to recall what probability they had attributed to each event, and the results showed that they believed they had attributed high probabilities to events that had occurred and lower ones if the event in question had not occurred because they thought they had always considered it unlikely.

There is thus the creation of a cognitive illusion as one reevaluates one's beliefs against what happened.

1.3 Errors of preference

Classical theory assumes that individuals can choose the solution that maximizes their utility and welfare because their preferences are well-defined and clear. In reality, empirical evidence highlights how these rules of rationality are broken and that these errors are connected with the effects I will illustrate in the following paragraphs.

1.3.1 Status quo

This type of bias is based on the preference of the current situation being identified as the reference point; conversely, any variation or change is considered a loss.

Research by two scholars (Samuelson and Zeckhauser, 1988) shows how subjects are inclined to the status quo. These were subjected to a problem: they were assigned an initial situation in which they were said to be serious readers interested in finance but with little money to invest. Then these received a large sum from a great uncle's inheritance and had to consider different portfolios and then decide whether to invest in low or high-risk securities, treasury bills, or bonds.

Another group of individuals, on the other hand, was asked the same problem but the amount being inherited was already partially invested. Studies done on these individuals confirm the effect of this bias, in that those who had inherited the entire liquid sum preferred to invest the money in securities with higher risk than those who had inherited the portfolio. It can be seen, then, that attachment to the status quo is increasingly higher as the number of options from which subjects must choose increases.

1.3.2 Certainty effect

The certainty effect is distorting from decision making, as it arises even if the probabilities are already known. Its consequences depend on the value of the probabilities themselves since they are calculated nonlinearly, but with variation according to their position in the range $(0,1)$.

Individuals assign excessive value to certainty; a change from a probability of 100% to one of 90% is more significant than a change from 50% to 40%. Certainty thus leads individuals to consider certain events likely and underestimate or even ignore events that are unlikely because they are considered impossible. Preferring certainty one is more inclined to the total elimination of risk rather than its reduction.

In this regard, an experiment was carried out (Kahneman and Tversky, 1979) in which an insurance policy was proposed that cost half as much as the ordinary policy, but that in the event of a claim would reimburse only 50% of cases; however, provision was made for the return of the entire premium if no settlement was made. This proposal was rejected by as many as 80% of respondents.

In conclusion, given the range (0,1) individuals tend to overestimate changes in probabilities if they affect extreme values while underestimating them for all other values.

1.3.3 Reflection effect

The reflex effect occurs in a situation of all-negative alternatives, as subjects prefer a probable loss rather than a certain loss even if of less value. In contrast to classical theory, gains and losses are not considered in the same way but vary depending on whether subjects refer to one or the other.

About this, it has been experimented (Kahneman and Tversky, 1983) that individuals placed in a position to choose between certain or probable gain opt for the certain gain, otherwise in the context of losses their propensity to risk rather than suffer a certain loss increases.

1.3.4 Isolation effect

To simplify a decision problem, the isolation effect results from decomposing a problem into its elements by then considering only a part of it and leaving out the common features.

Imagine a situation in which you have a choice to try to win:

A ($4,000 with probability 0.20) and B ($3,000 with probability 0.25)

In this first stage you have a probability of 0.75 of finishing the game without winning and a probability of 0.25 of continuing to the second stage, where you must make the following choice:

C ($3,000 certain) and D ($4,000 with probability 0.80)

In this second stage of the game, the choice is between two alternatives: winning an amount equal to $4,000 with a probability of 0.20 (0.25 x 0.80) and a chance of 0.25 (0.25 x 1.0) of winning $3,000 i.e., the same odds as in the first situation. However, Kahneman and Tversky show how in the first case individuals chose alternative A for 65 percent, while in the second situation alternative C was chosen for 78 percent of the sample cases. This happens because subjects tend to treat consecutive probabilities separately; in fact, research shows inconsistency in people's choices, which ignore probabilistic components.

1.3.5 Framing effect

Another phenomenon that can disprove the rationality hypothesis in decision making is the framing effect. This term is intended to explain how subjects' preferences vary depending on how the problem itself is presented. The way the information is presented and the language used to affect the decision maker, and from this comes logical and reasoning errors resulting in a simplified view of choice alternatives.

Framing can be by the subject agent or by the one who provides the information by diverting attention to a particular type of interpretation. The framing effect was demonstrated by Kahneman and Tversky through an analysis of the results derived from two groups of subjects who were presented with a situation where the United States would face a rare "Asian disease" that predicted 600 people would die. To deal with the state of emergency, the first group was asked to choose between two possible programs A and B.

Program A predicted that 200 people would be saved, while Program B predicted that with a 1/3 probability 600 people would be saved and with 2/3 no one would be saved. 72% of respondents chose alternative A.

The second group of people was always asked to choose between program A or B, but the two questions were asked differently.

Program A predicted that 400 people would die, Program B that none would die with a probability of 1/3, and 600 people would die with a probability of 2/3. In this case, most subjects chose alternative B. The explanation lies in the fact that the decision-making process is conditioned by the way the problem is presented, but a closer reading shows that the alternative A of the first problem is equivalent to alternative A of the second question, the same is true between the two alternatives B.

It, therefore, happens that individuals prefer a certain outcome therefore in the first case program A, on the contrary in the second situation in a negative perspective individuals are more risk-averse and therefore prefer alternative B.

The same effect underlies the results received from the study by McNeil Et Al (1982) in which two situations are presented that have the same statistical outcome relative to surgery, where physicians are more likely to avoid surgery if the outcome is proposed in terms of mortality.

Kahneman and Tversky explain that the order of preference among prospects should not depend on the way they are described. In particular, two versions of a problem that are recognized as equivalent when shown together should elicit the same preference even when shown separately.

In actuality, this requirement cannot be met because the choices vary with the form in which the problem is submitted, consequently, the convexity of the utility curve, which is not always a concave function, varies.

1.3.6 Disposition effect

Using the prospect, theory can be explained the disposition effect, which leads to immense portfolio movement. If a held security undergoes an appreciation, the investor is in the so-called earnings area, according to the theory mentioned earlier, thus in a situation where risk aversion prevails. Moreover, if the price of that security were to fall, it would create a disutility greater than the utility that an appreciation might generate. For these reasons, he will decide to sell the securities that will experience an upturn.

Conversely, if a stock were to generate a loss, he will be in the area of risk aversion and will prefer to keep stocks in the portfolio even if they lose. The realization of the loss will be postponed, although this might make one believe in a possible recovery because the mental account is not closed.

The investor will calculate losses concerning the money invested in the securities and not the overall wealth, finding it convenient to sell securities that have generated profit to buy securities that have depreciated. This logic worsens portfolio performance, moreover, "the disposition effect can affect market performance by acting as a counterweight to significant price increases or decreases. When prices fall, many investors who bought at higher prices will refrain from selling, helping to slow the fall in prices. When prices rise, profit-taking by investors who bought at lower prices will be a brake on price growth." (Rigoni, 2006)

1.4 The evolution of a new theory

Behavioral finance has set out to study the behavior of economic agents on the assumption that they may act irrationally. There are many scholars, such as Kahneman and Tversky, who analyze market anomalies and the way subjects make decisions characterized by errors or bias, resulting in a distortion of reality. Also contributing to choice bias are heuristics that are used in the collection and processing of information to facilitate choice.

All of the errors discussed so far, are derived from studies and research that have led to the demonstration of how the behavior of various individuals is contrary to traditional theories. Therefore, an attempt has been made to describe how individuals behave in decision making with the use of a new descriptive theory that will be covered in the next chapter, including the cumulative version. In this sense, prospect theory employs a different method, in that its purpose is not to indicate behavioral rules to be followed but to describe the attitudes of individuals.

Chapter 2
The descriptive theories of investment choice

Decision making under conditions of uncertainty can be analyzed from a normative or descriptive perspective. Expected utility theory is referred to as the normative approach and is considered the classical model for explaining choices under risky conditions, as it assumes absolute rationality in individuals. It also implies maximization of the utility function by predicting solutions consistent with the initial assumptions.

It is well known how psychological processes influence individuals, and for this reason, it was necessary to create a theory that would incorporate the decision problems of individuals under conditions of uncertainty. The first step toward this direction will be taken by varying the way economic theory is conceived, that is, through a descriptive approach.

This chapter will expound on a theory that explains how information processing occurs, illustrating irrational choice-making behaviors that counter the classical theory. Empirical research has also shown that even in the absence of rationality, one can still detect a certain frequency of responses in similar contexts.

The prospect theory will also be discussed below in its cumulative version, first presented by Daniel Kahneman and Amos Tversky (1979), which can be defined as an alternative to Von

Neumann and Morgenstern's model. The motivational approach will also be explored to highlight the departure from classical theory and the violation of rationality.

2.1. The Theory of Prospect

Prospect Theory was born in 1979 by Kahneman and Tversky with the intent to describe how individuals make decisions. The theory divides the choice process under uncertainty into two phases: the editing phase and the alternatives evaluation phase.

The editing phase precedes the moment of evaluation proper and is the stage in which the problem is reformulated and reorganized using cognitive filters to limit an excessive amount of information to be processed. Most errors are generated at this stage because the way the problem is proposed depends on the editing activity.

Six procedures that are part of this phase tend to be identified:

I. Encoding;

II. Combination;

III. Segregation;

IV. Deletion;

V. Simplification;

VI. Detection of dominance.

In Phase I of coding, individuals make an assessment based on a reference point. Kahneman and Tversky (1979) in this regard point out that gains and losses are defined by a reference point that usually corresponds to the current asset position, and that gains and losses coincide with amounts received or paid. This is because they believe that subjects are not able to evaluate absolute magnitudes, but rather differences from a starting point. For example consider a stock that gives an outcome worth $100, according to classical theory this outcome is the same for all individuals. In contrast, according to prospect theory, the security could have been purchased for $90 or $115, so the first individual would perceive a gain while the second would perceive a loss.

This stage is very relevant because it allows for the identification of subjective outcomes, as the choice of the reference point depends on several factors such as the framing of the problem, experiences, culture, and education of the subject. Proceeding with phase II, or the combination phase, allows us to associate probabilities of equal outcomes to obtain a single outcome.

In Phase III, segregation, the risky component can be identified and separated from the risk-free component.

Stage IV, cancellation, involves subjects canceling shared elements of problems. In this regard, Kahneman and Tversky provide an example in which they say that in the first stage of a game you have a 0.75 probability of nothing happening and a 0.25 probability of entering the second stage. The latter involves two games: in-game A there is a 0.8 probability of winning 4,000 dollars, or a 0.2 probability of losing; in-game B, on the other hand, there is a certainty of winning 3,000 dollars.

The choice has to be made a priori, and most subjects choose game B, as an elimination of the first stage of the game takes place and thus the problem arises as if it were a choice between a certain or random gain.

Step V, or simplification, is for individuals to tend to make rounding; an outcome of 101 with a probability of 0.49 will be considered as an outcome of 100 and a probability of 0.50. In addition, those events that are considered unlikely because they are considered impossible will be eliminated.

Finally, the last procedure is to remove the dominated alternatives, that is, those probability distributions that can be considered inferior to others. Having completed the editing phase, we proceed to the prospect evaluation phase in which the decision maker chooses the alternative with the highest value by comparing their simplified versions. The value is determined by referring to the value attributed to the outcomes (v)and the weighting of relative probabilities (π).

$$V = \sum_{i=1}^{N} \pi(p_i)v(x_i)$$

Where:

- ❖ pi - Is the probability of the i-th outcome
- ❖ xi - is the i-th outcome
- ❖ π (-) is the probability weighting function
- ❖ v (-) is the function of assigning the value of individual outcomes

Compared with the neoclassical utility function, there are some important differences: probabilities and outcomes are the results of the editing process that can generate changes in the available prospects, and outcomes are also not evaluated absolutely but as a difference from a reference point. The value function has the same role as the utility function but different characteristics and probabilities are weighted nonlinearly by the weighting function.

If the outcomes are all positive or negative, the certain component i.e., the minimum profit or loss that can be obtained is segregated. So the formula becomes:

$$V \qquad = v(x_j) + \sum_{i=1}^{N} \pi(p_i)(v(x_i) - v(x_j))$$

In conclusion, the value of the game found only in gains or losses is given by the sum of the value of the minimum gain or loss and the sum of the differences between the value of risky and certain, weighted outcomes.

Next, the two functions for calculating value in the evaluation phase will be analyzed in detail (Rigoni, 2006).

2.1.1 The value function

The purpose of the value function is to assign value to the outcomes of a game for the individual. This function is defined by changes in wealth relative to a reference point, and it does not have a linear trend but is concave in the region of gains and less steep than in the region of losses, where the function is convex instead. It also has a steeper slope in the vicinity of the reference point, small changes near the starting point impact more than large changes but are far from that point.

Figure 1 shows the value function of the prospect theory where the reference point can be identified at the intersection of the two axes.

Figure 1: The value function

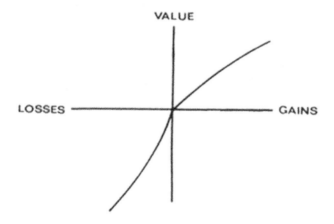

Such a representation has an "S" shape and is a simplification of reality. The two scholars Kahneman and Tversky argue that the value of an outcome depends not only on the gain or loss relative to the reference point but also on the reference point itself. A gain of $10,000 may be valued differently if the reference point is $100,000 or $1,000. This is why the previously proposed graph lacks one variable namely initial wealth, even though a change in wealth is considered more significant than starting wealth.

The concavity of the function in the area of earnings implies that for low levels of wealth the increase in earnings creates a larger effect, in fact, the difference between $1,000 and

$1,500 is greater than the difference between $50,000 and $50,500. This is because the person who has low wealth perceives the increase more than the one who already has a high level of wealth.

Depending on the context, risk aversion or risk propensity also varies, tending if that choice falls in the area of gains individuals are risk-averse while the moment one moves into losses a risk propensity is evidenced. These situations have been confirmed by empirical evidence, however, it is necessary to emphasize how the personal value function is influenced by the condition in which the individual finds himself or herself. It is likely that in certain regions of gain or loss the propensity turns into aversion because precisely the value function is modified by the specific circumstances.

Consider the following example:

Game A	
Probability	Outcome
0,2	-500.000 dollars
0,7	0

Game B	
Probability	Outcome
1	-100.000 dollars

It is well known that in the domain of losses, subjects are risk-averse and thus prefer risky alternative A rather than certain alternative B. However, if a loss of $500,000 has consequences that are too harmful to a subject, then the propensity will turn into aversion. This happens when losses are large and regions of concavity and risk aversion are created in the value function.

The possibility that the characteristics of the function are impaired in certain regions by circumstances cannot be ruled out. The reason why individuals are less satisfied when they win an amount of money than the displeasure they feel when they lose the same amount can be seen from the greater slope in the area of losses, i.e., to cover a loss it is necessary to have a greater gain.

2.1.2 Loss aversion and certain loss

The phenomenon previously illustrated, represents the so-called loss aversion analyzed by Kahneman and Tversky and represented graphically through the value function. Research shows that losses are 2-2.5 times more important than gaining the same amount. In other words, a gain of at least $200-250 will be needed to cover the displeasure suffered from a $100 loss (Cervellati,2012). This adversely affects investors who consequently make decisions that are not very rational, so much so that debt aversion can be generated in the financial sphere. While this can be seen as a benefit, it would create more financial disruption.

Instead, the concept of certain loss aversion refers to individuals taking greater risks to recoup a past loss. If a manager decides to undertake a risky investment because he believes that it may have prospects for growth in the future, should he be faced with the choice of whether or not to continue that project he will be reluctant to give up as he will want to avoid a certain loss. Moreover, even though it is evident that the project is far from profitable he will want to continue in the hope of returning to the break-even point.

2.1.3 Mental accounting

Kahneman and Tversky through the elaboration of prospect theory bring to light a critical aspect namely framing by outlining irrationality under conditions of choice. Framing effects refer to loss aversion and certain losses discussed earlier, and mental accounting. The latter leads individuals to reason by dividing their money into mental accounts by differentiating them into three categories: consumption, income, and wealth accounts.

All expenditures made are reported in the consumption accounts and are accounted for in such a way as not to cause displeasure.

In income accounts, sums of money are recorded according to how they were received, whether occasionally or not. The propensity to consume depends on the source from which the income is derived; if traceable to a lottery winning it will be spent more frivolously than the same amount but earned through salary.

About wealth, the valuation varies depending on the type of asset, which may be a current asset, financial investment, securities investment, or future collection.

Most individuals, therefore, make decisions according to a pyramidal process through which there is the creation of a kind of portfolio. Each level of such a pyramid corresponds to different needs or investment choices to be met. It is necessary, however, to have an overview of mental accounts to try to make the best use of mental accounting, since the resources intended to satisfy a need for gain have the same value as those intended to satisfy a need for protection.

2.1.4 The weighting function

The second function for calculating the value of the game in the evaluation stage is the weighting function, which represents the weight given to the value of each outcome. This weight does not coincide with the probability of the outcome but depends on it, also does not respect the rules of probability the sum of the weights is not inevitably equal to 1. From this it follows that in prospect theory, the value of a game is not linear concerning probability, contrary to classical theory.

The weighting function turns out to be an increasing function and $\pi(0)=0$, while $\pi(1)=1$ therefore impossible outcomes are ignored; in addition, over-weighting of the probability $\pi(p) > p$ occurs when the probability is small, in contrast, hypo-weighting occurs in the case where the probability is high and therefore $\pi(p)< p$. It is also called a sub-additive function for small probabilities, $\pi(rp)>r\pi(p)$ with $0< r< 1$, meaning for example that the weight of 0.01 to a probability is more than half the weight assigned to a probability of 0.02.

Finally we talk about disubstantiation, the so-called certainty effect for $0 < r < 1$ occurs $\pi(p) + \pi(1- p) < 1$. This means that subjects faced with uncertain events have an attitude that may be such that the sum of the weights associated with complementary events is less than the weight that is associated with a certain event. For this reason, the linearity principle inherent in expected utility theory is abandoned.

Figure 2 shows how the weighting function is represented graphically.

Figure 2: The weighting function

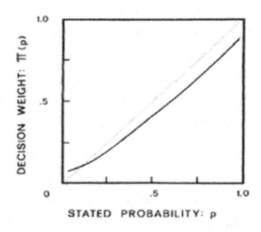

It can be seen from the graph that the probability values are always higher than the decision weights. Exceptions are the lowest values where over-weighting of probabilities occurs and the weights are higher.

Extreme values of probability lead to variable behavior of the weighting function because in the structuring phase, of which the prospect is the subject, some unlikely events may be considered impossible, and conversely very likely events are considered certain. Tying together choices and decision weights, instead of probabilities, makes it possible to explain several economic paradoxes among them the axiom of independence in Allais' paradox. Here subjects were asked to choose between Game A and Game B initially, and later between Game C and D.

Game A	
Probability	Outcome
0,33	2.500
0,66	2.400
0,01	0

Game B	
Probability	Outcome
1	2.400

Game C	
Probability	Outcome
0,33	2500
0,67	0

Game D	
Probability	Outcome
0,34	2.400
0,66	0

Using the utility function, subjects' choices can be expressed as follows:

The choice between A and B

$$U(2400) > 0.33U(2500)+0.66U(2400)$$
$$0.34U(2400) > 0.33U(2500)$$

The choice between C and D

$$0.33U(2500) > 0.34U(2400)$$

evident how the two choices are at odds with each other. Otherwise using prospect theory, the choices emerge as follows:

The choice between A and B

$$V(2400) > \pi\,(0,33)v(2500) + \pi(0,66)v(2400)$$
$$\frac{v(2400)}{v(2500)} > \frac{\pi(0,33)}{1 - \pi(0,66)}$$

The choice between C and D

$$\pi(0{,}33)v(2500) > \pi(0{,}34)v(2400)$$

$$\frac{\pi(0{,}33)}{\pi(0{,}34)} > \frac{v(2400)}{v(2500)}$$

Recapitulation results in:

$$\frac{\pi(0{,}33)}{\pi(0{,}34)} > \frac{v(2400)}{v(2500)} > \frac{\pi(0{,}33)}{1 - \pi(0{,}66)}$$

Where the sum of the decision weights of complementary events must be less than 1. From a purely economic view, it turns out that the independence axiom is not fulfilled by Allais' paradox because games C and D are derived from games A and B. Thus if game A is smaller than B, the same argument should hold for the other two games (C<D), instead subjects choose D rather than C and this is because B is transformed from a certain game to an uncertain one and the difference between B and D is greater than $\pi(0.66)v(2400)$. Instead, game A is uncertain and in the transformation, to game C there is the elimination of the probability of winning null which is hyper-weighted by the subjects being very low, so $\pi(0.66) v(2400)$ is greater than the difference between A and C.

Through the certainty effect and the hyper-weighting of probabilities, it is possible to explain Allais' paradox. Indeed, the idea of the certainty effect is that the transformations are different depending on whether one changes an alternative from certain to uncertain rather than intervening on already risky alternatives. This is difficult to explain through expected utility theory, hence the need to introduce a psychological solution.

Whereas in classical theory the utility function was used to infer an individual's attitude toward risk, in prospect theory this is determined by the value function and the combination with the weighting function. Consider graphs 1 and 2, where the value function is concave i.e., in the domain of gains the realization of a win for an individual is associated with modified higher or lower probabilities as in Figure 2.

Similar discussion for the domain of losses. For example, consider the points in the domain of gains where subjective probabilities are lower than objective probabilities; the concavity of the function and the underestimation of probabilities allows us to understand why individuals harbor risk aversion and underestimate uncertain prospect wins. Conversely in the loss domain, underestimating probability causes individuals to engage in risk-taking behavior.

If, on the other hand, subjective probabilities are greater than objective probabilities it causes the propensity for positive prospects to increase and for negative values to decrease, so winning as well as losing appear more likely than they objectively are (Levy, 1992).

2.2 Cumulative prospect theory

Cumulative prospect theory is an evolution of the prospect theory proposed by Kahneman and Tversky in 1992. The main innovation introduced concerns decision weights, whereas previously in prospect theory they depended on the probability of the single outcome, so gain or loss with equal probability had equal weight, in cumulative prospect theory various weighting functions are used and the weights depend on the cumulative probability distribution.

Decision weights are obtained through a logic similar to that of rank-dependent models, and the weight of a gain, if it is better than, will be:

$$\pi_i^+ = w^+\left(1 - F(x_{i+1})\right) - w^+(1 - F(x_i))$$

Where+ - represents the gain weighting function, F(-)is the cumulative likelihood function, and the outcome decision weight is given by the difference between the weighting function applied to the probability of obtaining an outcome equal to or greater than and the weighting function applied to the probability of a strictly better outcome.

The same is true in the case of getting the weight of a loss:

$$\pi_i^- = w^-\left(F(x_i)\right) - w^-(F(x_{i+1}))$$

Where– (-) represents the loss weighting function, and in addition, the decision weight of a loss is given by the difference between the weighting function applied to the probability of obtaining a negative outcome equal to or worse than and applied to the probability of obtaining a strictly worse outcome.

Thus, the value of a random prospect will be:

$$V = \sum_{i=1}^{n} \pi_i v(x_i)$$

Where are the decision weights for gains and losses.

a weighting function of gains and one of the losses was then formulated by the two scholars, where p denotes the cumulative probability:

$$w^+(p) = \frac{p^{0.61}}{(p^{0.61} + (1-p)^{0.61})^{1/0.61}}$$

$$w^-(p) = \frac{p^{0.69}}{(p^{0.69} + (1-p)^{0.69})^{1/0.69}}$$

Figure 3 is the representation of the cumulative probability weighting function.

Figure 3: The weighting function for gains and losses

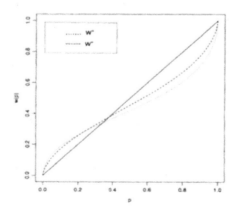

It can be seen from the figure that the sensitivity of decision weights is low when one is placed on intermediate probabilities, for example, the impact on the choice of a probability going from 40% to 41% is very small. In contrast, about probabilities that lie at the extremes the sensitivity increases, in fact the impact on choice is greater in the case where the probability goes from 1% to 2% as well as from 98% to 99%.

In contrast to what has been seen in prospect theory where individuals are considered risk-averse in the region of gains and risk-averse in the domain of losses, in cumulative prospect theory, it can be said that individuals are risk-averse at the time when gains are fairly likely and with a not large amount, instead they are risk-averse in the case when gains are unlikely and with a large amount.

To clarify the concept, let us consider two games with effects in the earnings domain:

Game A		
Weight		Value
+1 - + 0,05	= 1 - 0,13	V(0)
+0,005 -+ 0	= 0,13 - 0	V(2000) = 803,25

In game A there is a high payoff but a very low probability, in contrast in game B there is a high chance of winning a much smaller amount. If we use prospect theory to analyze these cases, individuals would be risk-averse because they would not accept either game without having with certainty 100. Whereas using cumulative prospect theory we can see that:

Game B		
Weight		Value
+ 1 - + 0,05 + 0,05 -+ 0	= 1 - 0,13 = 0,13 - 0	V(0) = 0 V(2000) = 803,25
Value of the game = 0,13*803,25 = 104,42		

Game B		
Weight		Value
+ 1 - + 0,05 + 0,95 -+ 0	= 1 - 0,79 = 0,79 - 0	V(0) = 0 V(105,27) = 60,20
Value of the game = 0,79 * 60,20 = 47,56		

The expected value is lower than the game value and higher than B, so subjects are risk-averse in the former case and risk-averse in the latter.

In contrast in the loss domain, subjects are risk-averse when faced with low and more likely losses instead they are risk-averse when faced with high and unlikely losses.

An example similar to the previous one but in the loss domain will be proposed below:

Game C	
Probability	Outcome
0,95	0
0,05	-2000
Expected value	-100

Game D	
Probability	Outcome
0,05	0
0,95	105,27
Expected value	-100

Game C		
Weight		**Value**
- 0,95 —- 0 - 1— - 0,95	= 0,85 — 0 = 1 — 0,85	V(0) = 0 V(-2000) = -1807,45
Value of the game = 0,15 * - 1807,54 = 271,13		

Game D		
Weight		**Value**
- 0,05 —- 0 - 1— - 0,05	= 0,11 — 0 = 1 — 0,11	V(0) = 0 V(-105,27) = -82,84
Value of the game = 0,89 * - 8 = -73,73		

The expected value is greater than the value of Game C and less than the value of Game B. Thus, if according to prospect theory individuals should turn out to be risk-averse in both cases, using cumulative prospect theory subjects turn out to be risk-averse in the first case and risk-averse in the second.

2.3 Motivational approach

It is well known how the behavioral theme affects individuals when choosing an investment, as rationality is lacking and they are prone to errors both in terms of the securities to be included in the portfolio and decisions concerning the financial markets.

In a context such as behavioral finance, investors tend to construct so-called behavioral portfolios as they are conditioned by heuristics and a range of errors. Among the inputs used to determine behavioral portfolio theory can be considered the two theories previously discussed and a more motivational strand in which Lopes' (1987) theory is included. According to this perspective, decisions are based on two factors: device and contextual.

The former indicates how the individual deals with risk, depending on whether the desire for safety or the desire for potentiality prevails. Lopes believes that in most individuals safety prevails over the desire for potentiality, thus treater importance is given to losses rather than gains.

The second factor, as well as the contextual one, relates to the goals that are intended to be achieved to assess which situation deserves more risk.

According to this method, subjects make decisions in such a way as to decrease the probability of losing the wealth goal defined based on security and empowerment desires. This goal results from giving greater weight to favorable rather than undesirable outcomes.

There are various types of examples concerning this criterion, in that a subject might believe that the contextual factor and the dispositional factor are oriented in the same direction; but it is also possible that they are at odds, i.e., risk aversion and risk predisposition are opposed to each other.

In the first case, an individual may choose a low-risk investment in such a way as to match both his desire for security and his aspiration that is lower than the expected return on available investments. Conversely, in the second case the one who has claims that are too high compared to the expected return of available investments, but who at the same time desires a secure condition, is faced with a decision problem: "Is it preferable to choose an investment that satisfies the desire for security or wealth?"

The motivational theory, therefore, develops within the field of psychology in that decisions are influenced by factors that animate the individual; in fact, choices according to this model would not be made through a mean-variance approach but by considering the probability that a goal is pursuable or not.

The main differences that can be seen from descriptive theories concern outcomes, in that compared with prospect theory where outcomes are not connected with probabilities, in the motivational approach it is believed that these on the contrary are closely connected. Furthermore, it is argued that the efficient frontier is generated from the relationship between the return and the probability that the target set by the subject is greater than the final wealth. In other words, the constitution of the frontier i.e., the set of portfolios that satisfies the subject's investment choices, is no longer carried out using the mean-variance approach, but depends on the personal aspirations of individuals; if these turn out to be too high, no portfolio will be able to ensure that the goal is achieved and therefore cannot be optimal. Indeed, it is a shared thought that investors should hold a set of variables that in reality turns out to be utopian, as combining security, liquidity, storability, and profitability is hardly conceivable.

The prerogative of the Italian investor is insufficient portfolio diversification, as most tend to use their money in a single investment solution, as the saver is directed toward seeking security and short-term returns. To differentiate his investments, therefore, he needs advice from specialized personnel, considering that the Italian level of financial education turns out to be rather low.

Nowadays it is essential to be aware of what influences investment decisions and behavioral biases to be able to manage them to limit alterations in the logical process. For this reason, in the following chapter, I have chosen to introduce the topic of asset management as well as the management of a person's savings by an intermediary who performs this type of specialized activity.

Asset management turns out to be an excellent way to reduce portfolio risk and thus lead the investor to achieve goals using the resources saved.

Chapter 3
Asset management

In the present chapter, it was decided to analyze the issue of managed savings, since it could be seen earlier that many investors are inclined to save.

Asset management is a type of investment implemented mainly by savers who entrust their money to a financial intermediary specializing in its management if they feel they lack sufficient knowledge. These companies take the name of asset management companies, commonly called asset management or brokers. They professionally and institutionally carry out an 'activity of buying and selling real or financial assets based on a mandate, through which the person appointed will be responsible for creating in his name but on behalf of the client, a diversified portfolio that is consistent in terms of risk and return with the contract.

In this chapter I will attempt to define the essentials of the financial sphere by dwelling on the main instruments of asset management, from simple mutual funds, moving on to asset management, and finally Exchange Trade Funds, all after outlining the role of asset management companies. This will be followed by a definition of the concept of benchmarks in to enhance the references introduced in the explanation of financial instruments, then concluding with the fiscal framework to which they are subjected.

3.1. Asset management companies and their role

There are various financial intermediaries authorized for asset management, the main ones will be explained below and their functions defined. First, there are asset management companies commonly called asset management. They must also meet the requirements of professionalism, honorability, and independence of individuals who serve as directors, while only a requirement for shareholders to be of good standing is required. Their role is to create mutual funds to manage the savings of individuals.

The task of the asset management company is to carry out buying and selling of financial assets to create a more or less diversified portfolio according to the level of risk and return chosen by investors and the company itself. Of course, the management company is paid a fee on the activity performed, which goes to reduce the return obtained from the initial investment of individual savers.

Another type of intermediary is banks i.e., institutions that can raise and grant financial resources to individuals. They raise funds in two ways: through the direct method, that is, by issuing their liabilities using current accounts, bonds, and certificates of deposit. Or through the indirect method which in turn is divided into: administered savings, managed savings, and insurance products. The former includes custodial and escrow securities deposits, the latter includes mutual funds and asset management, and finally the latter include life insurance policies and pension funds.

Another type of intermediary is brokers i.e., securities professionals who professionally perform investment services on an individual basis for both their account and for third parties.

They carry out the asset management business on a customized basis for their clients, and also offer financial instrument trading services in regulated markets.

Usually, a saver relies on intermediaries because he or she does not have sufficient knowledge of financial economics, thus implementing the technique of diversification. According to a Bank's survey of 2,500 adults showing that only 37% of those who participated are familiar with the benefits of diversified investing.

Figure 4: The diversification of investments

Diversification

Individual investment   collective investment

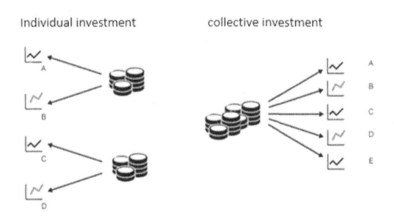

The diversification technique is useful in that a single investor has limited capital at his disposal, while the intermediary having much more liquidity at his disposal, has the opportunity to make investments in various funds obtaining a higher return and consequently reducing risk. The level of risk is defined using a benchmark called the benchmark, which will be discussed in more detail in the next section.

3.2 The benchmark

The term benchmark means the point of reference; in financial economics, it is an objective parameter calculated based on one or more financial indices, the value of which represents the risks associated with the performance of the mutual fund.

In a business context, the term benchmarking, refer to the activity of comparing a company with other competitors in the same industry to define its strengths and weaknesses. More specifically in a financial sense, the benchmark is a notional portfolio, i.e., a benchmark index representing a particular market with which you compare your portfolio. In other words, the benchmark is a portfolio that represents the weight and composition of those financial assets present in savers' real portfolios.

A benchmark is a tool that allows fund managers to define the investments to be implemented, making this index fundamental to the client and has made it a more democratic and publicly useful tool. Its usefulness consists precisely in providing an idea about the type of investment to be made and the management of the company. It's also able to provide an assessment of the market risk in which the portfolio is invested and the performance achieved relative to the benchmark index itself.

The benchmark takes on a different configuration depending on whether one looks at it from the perspective of the manager or the fund subscriber. From the manager's point of view, it represents the main information on which to base their decisions. Managers are rewarded based on the number of positive deviations they manage to make from the benchmark index.

Therefore, the benchmark must be very representative of the market in which it is intended to invest since an incorrect definition would create over-performance, valuation bias on management, and suboptimal portfolios.

As far as the investor is concerned, the benchmark represents the added value that the management of his or her portfolio has generated and the evaluation of the work done by the manager. This tool also makes it possible to define the risk level of the investment and to select the classes of financial investments to be considered in the creation of the portfolio.

The use of the benchmark to manage an investment, therefore, has multiple advantages among them an objective assessment of the investment itself by the subscriber, knowledge of the returns that can be achieved about the risk and time frame chosen, also an indication of the instruments and markets in which the fund invests and its valuation.

This index can represent the performance of a real portfolio that has the same composition in terms of the type of investment and geographical area of reference. Another element detected consists of its volatility from which it is possible to deduce the level of risk, that is, how the performance of the portfolio varies even though it is closely related to the type of investment made.

Finally, it is possible to make predictions about what the performance of the actual portfolio might be based on the performance of the benchmark portfolio and its risks. Once data on investment returns have been obtained, a comparison can be made with the benchmark to assess the correctness of investment choices and policies.

To give a practical example, let us consider a portfolio of U.S. bonds yielding a rate of 2 percent, which in absolute terms could lead to a positive valuation. However, if the U.S. bond market over the same period generated a yield of 4% then our considerations are no longer to be considered positive in that the fund manager did not seize all the opportunities that the market made available. This causes the portfolio to be negatively valued relative to the reference market.

The benchmark can consist of one or more financial indices, one index if you have a single reference market, multiple indices if referring to multiple markets or sectors then each is assigned a weight and then unified into a single index. We can therefore see it as a summary statistical measure that depicts the portfolio equivalent to the general performance of a specific market.

Another key feature of this index is that it is not static in that each type of fund allows managers a wide operating margin. This will involve adjustments to the benchmark to keep it in line with the investment at all times, monitoring the movements of stocks in the portfolio, and adjusting the benchmark index promptly to best portray the investment policy.

Underlying all these concepts are two factors namely risk and time frame from which the whole analysis of the reference index should disregard. One of the most frequent mistakes is to start from the return one wants to get from that investment, instead, the process should be the opposite in that the investor should ask himself: what level of risk do I intend to bear?

Once you can answer, then you can identify the assets that hold that requirement, and only then can you focus on maximizing the return.

The concept so far takes into account the returns of a virtual portfolio that differs from a real portfolio i.e. that of a mutual fund, the benchmark then is calculated and used as a simple yardstick.

3.3 The instruments of asset management

A real portfolio represents the preferences and needs of savers, in the market there are a great many financial instruments, more or less complex, made available by financial intermediaries. These instruments have very different purposes, functionalities, returns and risks. It is essential to search for the most appropriate instrument, with reference to one's needs; in particular, to choose the instrument that best suits the preferences of each saver, it is necessary to have a general knowledge of all the instruments in the market. This section will explain the various types of asset management, starting with mutual funds and continuing with asset management and Exchange Trade Funds.

3.3.1 Mutual funds.

3.3.1.1 Definition.

The main instrument of asset management is the mutual fund. A mutual fund is a collective asset composed of the savings of a plurality of savers, which is invested in securities such as government securities, foreign bonds, and Italian and non-Italian stocks, by asset management companies. The purpose of such investment is to obtain benefits from the point of view of returns and reduced management costs, increasing the bargaining power of the investment and obtaining a well-diversified portfolio.

The portfolio is allocated among subscribers in units, that is, the individual saver purchases units of that fund whose value (Net Asset Value) is disclosed daily. It is necessary to emphasize that the resources deployed by the subscribers constitute assets that differ from that of the company.

In general, mutual funds can be actively managed so they are characterized by asset management companies implementing buying and selling actions to beat the market. Otherwise, passively managed funds are linked to the benchmark to repeat their performance and contain their costs. Usually, an asset management company to told up a portfolio of securities to invest in funds must adopt several strategies in addition to using analysis.

First, it uses an asset allocation strategy to choose which securities to include in the portfolio by adhering to the fund rules; in addition, the choice may be based on the geographic area, sector, and capitalization of the companies selected by the fund. Another strategy is stock picking as well as an analysis of companies' histories and balance sheets to select the stocks to hold in the portfolio which is particularly characteristic of actively managed funds.

Finally, market timing i.e., the right timing needed to enter the markets at the time when there is expected to be an upturn or conversely the exit from the market in case a downturn is expected.

3.3.1.2 The classification of mutual funds.

There are various types of mutual funds in the market, both actively managed and passively managed, subdivided according to the variable to be considered. A first distinction can be made between income distribution and income accumulation. One speaks of a fund with the distribution of income if this has as its objective the crediting of capital gains to its subscribers, on the basis of predetermined periods without forgetting that we are not talking about fixed income but random and variable as it derives from a kind of corporate profit.

Moreover, to enhance the value of the units, a part of such capital gains may be allocated to the fund's capital. In contrast, income-accumulation funds are funds that retain all earnings internally to be invested again, so that an increase in capital and a consequent increase in units will be generated. Monetary gains will be realized by the saver only at the time of disinvestment.

Taking another variable into consideration, we can divide funds into two other types that allow us to define those that hold fixed or variable assets, classifying them into closed-end and open-end funds. The former is characterized by a predetermined amount of units that do not vary over time. The subscription of such funds takes place on fixed dates, and in addition, the right of redemption can be made only at maturity.

A typical feature of closed-end funds is that they have a long-term time horizon with a higher entry-amount than other funds, which is why it is a widely used instrument in the securities sector. Typical investment cases in these funds may be venture capital or development and rehabilitation with turna-round maneuvers in enterprises.

As for open-ended funds, they can be said to have greater flexibility in that units can be subscribed to or redeemed at any time. To determine the value of a unit, being precisely a variable fund, the calculation is done daily by simply doing the ratio between the Nav (Net Asset Value) value and the number of units outstanding.

They usually invest in listed financial assets and are much more popular than a closed-end fund because of their simplicity and flexibility. Since they are widely used, it should be noted that there are various types of open-end funds: harmonized and non-harmonized open-end funds, equity funds, bond funds, balanced funds, and money market funds. (Liera, 2005)

Open-end funds are mutual funds that are managed by asset management companies. This type of fund is subject to less stringent rules so that this turns into greater freedom of investment. It can be seen that these main funds are speculative.

Then there are equity funds that invest at least 70 percent in equities and are useful for growing capital over a long period from 7-10 years and beyond. Equity funds have riskiness that increases with increasing specialization and are less volatile when diversified across multiple countries. The maximum remaining 30 percent of the portfolio, can be invested in bonds or cash.

In contrast, in bond funds, it is not possible to invest in stocks and therefore one must invest the money entirely in bonds and cash. They are useful for those who need to grow their capital over 3 to 5 years. The longer the average maturity of the bonds in the portfolio, the greater the volatility of bond funds. This type of fund is classified based on two criteria: the market risk they take on by investing, based on financial duration and currency, and credit risk, that is, depending on the issuer, country, and creditworthiness.

On the other hand, we speak of balanced funds in the case where one can invest in both stocks and bonds. Balanced funds can be bond funds in case the capital is invested more in bonds with a percentage ranging from 10 percent to 50 percent in equities, otherwise they are equity balanced funds if the majority of the investment is in equities, thus for a percentage ranging from 50 percent to 90 percent. The purpose of such funds is to allow more flexibility without having to choose one of your types illustrated above.

In conclusion, there are money funds i.e., a type of fund that is low risk but also low reward. They are so called precisely because of their extreme liquidity, and they invest assets in short-term instruments such as bonds or securities of State with a duration of less than one year. A special feature of such funds is that securities are usually purchased in dollars to obviate exchange rate risk, although there are money funds that invest in other currencies.

3.3.1.3 The costs of mutual funds.

A much-discussed dynamic these days concerns the mutual fund costs that savers face. There are mainly two types of expenses they face: recurring fees and one-time fees. Essentially the latter are charged at the time of purchase or sale and are amortized as the time spent in the fund passes; they are called entry fees, are paid by the fund to the broker and then deducted from the amount subscribed by the investor. In contrast, exit fees are deducted from redemption. Those funds that do not charge either type of fee are called pure no-loads.

Different, however, are the incentive fees that are given to the fund manager for managing to beat the market as a kind of extra return. This process is complicated because since the benchmark is an average of stock returns, even if the gross returns obtained by the manager were to be equal these will be reduced by costs that lead to lower returns making them still lower than the benchmark.

In conclusion, there are brokerage fees-that is, costs for buying and selling individual securities. This means that they will be higher the more operational the fund is, therefore they will affect the price of the security.

3.3.2 Asset management

Asset management is a form of investment that allows savers to entrust their assets to a professional, mediated by a mandate contract. In this case, the investment is managed separately for each client, being a particularly personalized investment service each portfolio differs from the others. It is defined by the manager who together with the client's needs goes on to create an optimal portfolio that reflects the risk profile and investment objectives.

These financial products are created to meet the interests of major investors.

Securities asset management is a mandate contract under which Asset Management or brokers engage in buying and selling transactions for and on behalf of clients, and their assets are used to purchase stocks and/or bonds. In order to determine the percentage of equity securities or funds that can be placed in the management, different risk ranges must be defined. The most common are the bond, balanced, and equity lines. In the bond one the investments focus on bonds to have more security, in the balanced line the investments are diversified between bonds and equities, and in the equity line they focus mainly on equities. This type of investment because it is an individual investment, requires a high minimum amount so that the manager has the opportunity to create a properly diversified portfolio to minimize risk. To give the investment strategies a chance to generate a high result, a medium to long time period is required.

As for fund-based asset management, these are financial products that invest in mutual funds . It is a service that allows the constitution of a well-diversified portfolio of investments, that is, with instruments that possess different characteristics, as the investment is made in several funds. Its main objective is to enable even the smallest savers to access a diversified portfolio by choosing from various investment lines the dynamic, balanced or prudent one.

The dynamic line involves investment within equity funds with the option of purchasing both shares of asset management companies and international investment companies.

The balanced line plans to invest the assets partly in equities and partly in bond funds.

In conclusion, the prudent line, involves investing mainly in funds bonds and only to a small extent in equity funds.

We are therefore in the presence of a product that can be defined as a synthesis of other products already present, which takes on its own risk and return profile. The fact that they consist of diversification translates into an advantage, while the factor that makes the use of these instruments unpalatable is their cost since in addition to management fees, there are also those that accrue to the fund manager so the investor will receive a lower return.

3.3.3 Exchange Traded Funds

A particular type of mutual funds are ETFs better known as Exchange Traded Funds, whose shares are traded like stocks in regulated markets. Unlike normal mutual funds, their shares are determined according to supply and demand at any given time and not at the end of each day. Such funds refer to an index i.e., the instrument that allows one to track market performance by proposing an average of all stocks in the market to check the general state of the stock market or of a particular sector or geographic area; they then replicate the performance to achieve excellent results in terms of both cost reduction and portfolio diversification. In addition, they hold relatively low management costs, when compared with those of other mutual funds, but which still make the performance lower than that of the benchmark. Traders are then required, with the aim of making the ETF market more liquid, to issue letter orders to sell units and cash orders to buy units, with a differential and frequency that are determined by the American Stock Exchange.

As was previously explained ETFs replicate an index, and this replication can be done in four different ways. The full physical replication mode consists of buying all the securities included in the index in order to be aligned with the index at all times. Since it is a passively managed fund, the manager will only have to deal with the buying and selling of securities so that the weights remain the same in relation to changes in the index. Another mode is physical replication by sampling i.e., the purchase of securities to be held in the portfolio in smaller quantities, trying to replicate the characteristics of the index that can make it perform as well as it does.

On the other hand, unfunded synthetic replication is when ETFs use sums from subscriptions to purchase securities and by creating a swap contract usually with a bank, which can guarantee a rate that equals that of the reference index. In addition, to guarantee the subscriber, the fund insures the purchase of up to 10 percent of the Nav in derivative instruments.

Finally, synthetic replication funded, whereby the fund enters into a swap contract with a counterparty. It gives the fund the return of the benchmark index in exchange for the cash contribution that comes from subscribing to the units. The risk arises from the fact that the fund's entire assets are allocated to the fund and thus there is an absence of diversification. To overcome this, it is necessary to place securities as collateral in the name of the counterparty but in favor of the fund, for a value exceeding 100 percent of the value of the Nav.

When you decide to buy an ETF, you can access various investment categories based on the benchmark to which they relate. They can in fact replicate bond indices if they invest in government bonds or bonds of private companies that belong to the dollar zone or internationally. They can also replicate equity indices, that is, indices that hold an equity portfolio most often broken down by sector, geographic area or size of the company in which they intend to invest. But there are also index ETFs that replicate indices of real estate companies or commodities in case they peg to the trend of their value.

Beyond indexed ETFs there is a particular category the structured ETFs, which aim to safeguard the portfolio, amplify returns or make more complex investments using a variety of strategies. By associating the liability that characterizes ETFs with different portfolio strategies, it is allowed even the smallest savers to invest at reduced prices in elaborate strategies, as they do not have entry and exit costs.

With reference to the type of strategy to be adopted these funds are divided into: ETFs with protection, with leverage, short with or without leverage, and with covered call or buy-write.

Protection ETFs take advantage of the rise in the benchmark index by insuring the value of the portfolio from any market fallout. Leveraged ETFs use instruments that multiply the outcome by generating leverage, aiming for a return that is more than proportional to the index they refer to. Short ETFs, on the other hand, use an inverse market participation strategy, meaning that they sell the securities they buy. Finally, ETFs with a covered call strategy involve buying securities replicating the chosen benchmark and selling a call option on the fund shares themselves with the right to buy at a price greater than 5 percent the ETF.

In conclusion, it can be said that ETFs are much more efficient when compared to mutual funds because the costs referred to the latter are far greater. In fact, ETFs being passive funds and replicating a benchmark do not hold brokerage costs, other than those referring to the opening of the fund itself and maintaining alignment with the index. For this reason, the Exchange Trade Funds market is considered much more competitive in terms of cost efficiency.

By considering the characteristics of the various types of investments, it is possible to analyze the advantages and disadvantages of each financial choice.

So far, types of asset management have been analyzed; in fact, mutual funds, asset management and ETFs have been discussed, explaining the characteristics of each category.

By studying in detail how asset management is classified, it is possible to define its variants and costs, so that each investor can create his or her own well-diversified portfolio tailored to his or her needs, however, it could be seen that due to individuals' lack of financial knowledge it is necessary to entrust the management of their savings to professionals. This is to avoid incurring the previously illustrated errors: mental shortcuts i.e. the so-called "heuristics," cognitive and emotional and preference errors, which influence investment decisions by leading individuals to enact erroneous behavior as a result of a lack of financial knowledge.

We have only been able to analyze all these aspects on a theoretical level, but in order to test whether subjects are actually prone to making mistakes that then spill over into financial decisions, a statistical survey was prepared with the aim of studying the behavior of the subjects surveyed.

In the next chapter, therefore, two types of analysis will be exposed: a descriptive one by which the characteristics of the sample will be described, and a more specific one that will detect the errors that subjects are predisposed to make, with the aim of enhancing the biases exposed in the first two chapters.

Chapter 4
The analysis of behavioral errors

In the previous chapters, various behavioral, cognitive and emotional and preference errors were analyzed; in addition, the so-called heuristics that guide individuals in their choice processes were explained. The second chapter discussed descriptive theories of investment choice as well as prospect theory and a cumulative version of it and a more motivational approach.

Numerous empirical evidences show that many people are saving, unfortunately, the level of financial education is often very low , so a lot of mistakes are made at the level of management or simply in choosing the most appropriate form of savings for the individual person.

The theoretical excursus conducted so far will be useful for understanding the work carried out in this fourth chapter. In this regard, it was intended to concretize through empirical work what has been described so far, which is why this last chapter will be developed from a questionnaire consisting of 18 multiple-choice questions identified by me on the basis of the theoretical and empirical literature analyzed.

The first questions in the questionnaire are biographical questions, to analyze the general information of the individuals who filled out the questionnaire. Then it is composed of more specific, financial questions, which made it possible to carry out all the analyses necessary to detect the errors that characterize the sample and to find the financial education and knowledge of individuals. The economic-financial questions were collected from various studies such as those compiled by Consob, Kahneman and Tversky, Frederik, Lusardi, and Mitchell.

This questionnaire was created using ideal software for its implementation, called Qualtrics. For its distribution, the link was shared through the main social networks: Instagram, Facebook and Whatsapp so as to be able to reach a considerable sample of people.

Then the questionnaire was circulated and subsequently all the results obtained were downloaded, processed and analyzed, where various considerations could be made on a sample of 79 subjects who contributed to the full compilation, belonging to various age groups more precisely from 18 years to 70 and therefore with different backgrounds and skills.

The processing phase was divided into two types of analysis: an initial descriptive analysis aimed at illustrating the composition of the sample. Here all data were illustrated in the form of tables and graphs to give a complete representation.

The first data studied in this analysis were the subdivision:

- ❖ By gender of the sample;
- ❖ By age of the sample;
- ❖ By education level;
- ❖ By work situation;
- ❖ By perception of risk;

For economic and financial knowledge studied on the basis of four questions

formed by me for this study.

This is the starting point from which the characteristics of the participating subjects emerged, which will then be used in the subsequent analysis to provide justification for certain behavioral choices.

In fact, the following analysis, aims to compare with the previous theories studied, in order to carry out a verification and seek confirmation of the concepts set forth in the previous chapters.

4.1 Descriptive analysis

The first analysis that has been carried out is a descriptive one, to make the composition of the sample known. Various pieces of information about the individuals to whom the questionnaire was submitted will be provided, with the aim of using them at a later stage for the reworking of the data from the analysis of the errors that characterize individuals in their investment choices.

The purpose of this analysis is to learn about the gender, age{, level of education and employment status that characterizes

[69]

the sample. In addition, it was decided to analyze the subjects' level of economic-financial knowledge through four questions. The first one assumes knowledge of the main financial instruments, the second one is about the use of one's savings, and the third and fourth are about the interest rate and inflation. The latter two are proposed based on the questions carried out by Lusardi and Mitchell , as financial literacy has acquired relevance and is a relevant tool for making choices that affect wealth and enable people's well-being to be increased.

Financial knowledge is considered necessary to reduce the risk of making wrong decisions, particularly when the area concerns choices that project over the long term such as retirement savings. The moment individuals use only common sense to make a decision, they are misled as this is not sufficient; they need a minimum basic knowledge of the financial instruments in the market.

It was then decided to also analyze the risk appetite of the respondents based on how much agreement the subjects are in reference to a given statement, and then go on to make a comparison with the level of financial knowledge and see what correlation there is between these two variables.

4.1.1 The gender of the sample

The sample consisted of 34 men and 45 women, 43% and 57%, respectively, out of the total of 79 subjects.

Gender		
Men	34	43%
Women	45	57%
Total	79	100%

Gender of the sample

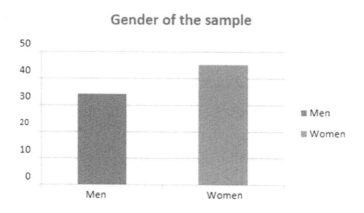

It can be seen that as age {increases, the composition of the sample also varies; in fact, in the age group between 18 and 30 as well as the largest, comprising 80 percent of the sample, the remainder consists of 6 percent of individuals between the ages of 31 and 50 and finally 14 percent of individuals over 51.

Regarding the gender composition of the various age groups {it can be seen that in the first two the sample is predominantly composed of women about 60 percent, while in the third bracket men make up the majority 73 percent, and women the remaining 27 percent.

[71]

The distinction of gender by age						
Age	Risk-averse		Men		Women	
18-30	63	80.00%	24	38%	39	62%
31-50	5	6.00%	2	40%	3	60%
51-70	11	14.00%	8	73%	3	27%
Total	79	100%	34		45	

4.1.2 The age of the sample

This sample was then divided according to the age{ of the respondents, including specifying how many of the respondents were men and how many were women. The range of respondents' age{ ranges from 18 to 69 years, the mean age{ is 28 years, and the median is 21 years. It can be seen that there is an imbalance in the sample regarding the age range of 20 to 22 years, which accounts for 70 percent of the sample, this to be kept in mind also in the considerations that will be made later. It can also be seen that the median age{ of women (25 years) is lower than that of men (31 years).

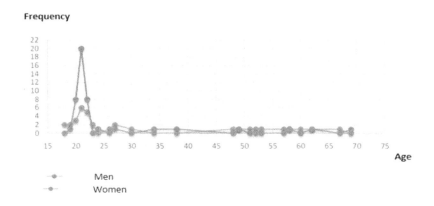

Sample age

Frequency

Age

- Men
- Women

4.1.3 The level of education

Subsequently, the sample was divided on the basis of the educational qualification held by the respondents, and it was found that 63 subjects, or 80 percent held a diploma, 7 subjects held a middle school diploma or lower qualification, or 9 percent of the total, there were then 5 subjects who held a master's degree i.e. 6 percent, and finally, 4 people held a bachelor's degree which corresponds to 5 percent of the respondents.

Education level		
	Total	%
Middle school diploma or lower	7	9%
High school diploma	63	80%
Bachelor's degree	4	5%
Master's degree	3	6%
Total	79	100%

Sample education level

5% 6% 9%

80%

4.1.4 Work situation

The sample was divided according to the employment status of each subject, the majority of the respondents (58%) i.e. 46 people state that they are students, this confirms the fact that the sample is composed of a group of people with a rather low average age {as well as predominantly college students.

8% of the sample corresponding to 6 people declared themselves self-employed

while 20% corresponding to 16 people are employees.

The remaining part of the sample includes 5% or 4 people who declare themselves unemployed and finally 9% or 7 people who declare themselves retired.

[74]

Work situation		
	Total	%
Student	46	58%
Self-employed	6	8%
Employee	16	20%
Unemployed	4	5%
Pensioner	7	9%
Total	79	100%

Work situation

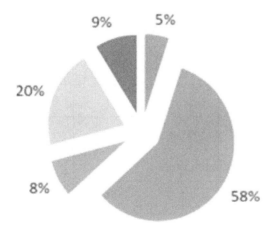

4.1.5 Perception of risk.

In order to analyze the perception of risk among the subjects, I decided to divide the sample based on the answers that were given to the question in which they were asked to indicate how much they agreed with the phrase "A risk is an uncertain event, with respect to which one should seek protection instead of a profit opportunity"(Consob). Respondents were to answer by indicating a value between 1 and 5, where 1 corresponds to "not at all agree" and 5 "very agree." On the basis of these responses, I considered those respondents who were inclined to risk to be either not at all agree or little agree, with a moderate profile if they responded with 3 i.e. "agree" and finally risk-averse those who responded with 4 or 5 i.e. "quite agree" and "very agree."

Perception of risk

Perception of risk		
	Total	%
Inclined to risk	26	33%
Moderate tolerance	33	42%
Risk-averse	20	25%
Total	79	100%

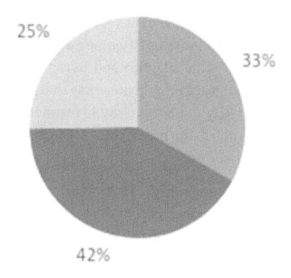

As can be seen from the graph and table, the risk-prone subjects numbered 26 or 33% of the total, the moderately tolerant subjects numbered 33 corresponding to 42% as well as the majority compared to the total sample. Finally, the risk-averse were found to be 20 or 25% of the sample. In contrast from the survey conducted by Consob (2019), 76% of the survey subjects turn out to be risk-averse. This divergence stems from the fact that the sample, participant in the survey I conducted, is very small.

Elaborating further on the data, it was found that most of the male component is risk-prone (41%) which corresponds to 14 men out of 34 total, while as for women only (27%) which corresponds to 12 women out of 45 are risk-prone. From this analysis it can be easily guessed that a man is roughly twice as likely to be risk-taking as a woman.

The analyzed sample also shows that risk-averse men corre-
spond to the 29% or 10 men out of 34, while risk-averse women
are 22% which corresponds to 10 women out of 45 total. In fact,
studies conducted by Jianakoplos and Bernasek (1996) show
that it is women who are more risk-averse than men in that the
latter are more likely to accept risky investments; this difference in results is due to the numerosity of the reference sample
and its composition.

Finally, in moderate tolerance, the sample analyzed shows that
29% of men corresponding in absolute value to 10 out of 34 total have moderate tolerance. As for women, we find a very high
percentage of 51% corresponding to 23 women out of 45 in the
total sample.

In conclusion, it is easy to see from this analysis that there is a
high risk appetite on the part of men, while most women have
a moderate profile.

Perception of risk by gender

Perception of risk		
	Total	%
Inclined to risk	26	33%
Moderate tolerance	33	42%
Risk-averse	20	25%
Total	79	100%

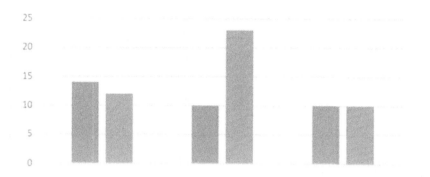

It is also interesting to note that by dividing the sample into three age groups between 18 and 30 years prevails an average tolerance of risk (41%) as well as in the range between 31 and 50 years old although slightly more (60 percent), while between 51 and 70 years old there is more risk-averse (55 percent). In general, it is difficult to determine which of the three categories is more risk-prone or risk-averse since most of the respondents are concentrated in the first age group, consisting of as many as 63 people, consequently, the results could also be biased. It can be seen, however, that the most risk-averse individuals are over 50 years of age. By relating the absolute value of the risk propensities i.e., 20 people with the risk averters 17 people in the first age group, it goes to create a ratio that is about 1:1, while always relating the inclined subjects i.e. 6, with the averse ones i.e. 1, but in the last age group the ratio changes and becomes 6:1.

Perception of risk by age

Perception of risk by age						
	18-30 years	%	31-50 years	%	51-70 years	%
Risk takers	20	32%	0	0%	6	55%
Moderate tolerance	26	41%	3	60%	4	36%
Risk-averse	17	27%	2	40%	1	9%
Total	63	100%	5	100%	11	100%

Perception of risk by age

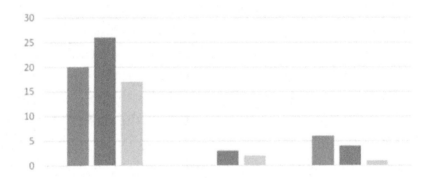

4.1.6 Economic knowledge

I decided to divide the sample according to the level of economic knowledge, using the following criterion: those subjects with high knowledge were placed among the high knowledge subjects who stated that they knew more than five financial instruments including checking account, savings account, bonds, stocks, government bonds, pension funds, futures and swaps.

Among the instruments chosen must be stocks and bonds since I assume that a high knowledge subject must be familiar with these two well-known types of investments.

Also holding high knowledge are those individuals who have invested their savings, as this assumes a greater knowledge of the financial market than those who have only deposited the money in the checking account, and finally those who have correctly answered two questions: the first referring to the interest rate: "Suppose you have 100 dollars in a savings account with a rate of 2% per year.

After 5 years, how much money do you think you will have in that account? " and the second to inflation: "Suppose your account has an interest rate of 1% per year and inflation is at 2% per year. After one year with that money, you will be able to buy a quantity of goods: less or more than you do today? ".

The proposed answers for the first question are: more than 102, less than 102, or don't know, obviously "More than 102" was the correct answer. As for the second question, the correct answer was "Less than today" (Lusardi and Mitchell, 2008). In contrast, those who know at least five financial instruments, including stocks and bonds, who, as far as their savings are concerned, can deposit them in a checking account, invest them or not save but who answered incorrectly at least one or both of the questions referring to interest rate and inflation showed an average level of knowledge.

I have also chosen to place in this category individuals who precisely invest in financial instruments but who answered the questions on inflation and interest rate incorrectly because I assume that an individual who invests his or her money should be aware of such basics as interest rate and inflation.

Finally, I identified subjects with poor knowledge-that is, those who knew less than five financial instruments and who answered one or both questions incorrectly. From these considerations made, the following data resulted:

10 are those with high knowledge (13%), 40 those with medium knowledge

(51 percent) and 29 with poor knowledge (37 percent).

Level of economic knowledge

Level of economic knowledge		
	Total	%
High knowledge	10	13%
Medium knowledge	40	51%
Poor knowledge	29	37%
Total	79	100%

Economic knowledge level

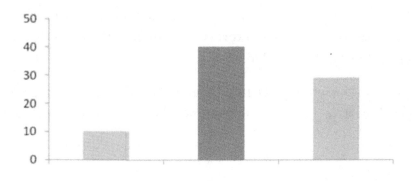

Next, I divided the sample between men and women by allocating them into the three different levels of knowledge. From this I noticed how men have more economic knowledge than women, in fact among those in the high knowledge category 60 percent are men and 40 percent are women. In contrast, the latter are far more numerous among those with medium and low knowledge.

It is evident how women compose about 69% of all those who hold poor knowledge, while men only 31% in fact we are talking about 20 women against 9 men. These data are also confirmed by other studies showing that women hold a lower level of financial knowledge than men, in fact the survey published in the first issue of Allianz's International Pension Papers, showed that men's responses were 31 percent better than women's (Lo Conte, 2017).

While among those with average knowledge were found to be 19 men and 21 women corresponding to 47.5 percent and 52.5 percent, respectively.

Knowledge level by gender

Perception of risk by gender					
	Males	%	Females	%	Total
High knowledge	6	60%	4	40%	10
Average knowledge	19	48%	21	53%	40
Poor knowledge	9	31%	20	69%	29
Total	34		45		79

Knowledge level by gender

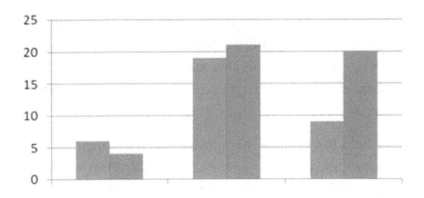

Next, I divided those with high, medium, and low knowledge according to age {range. As can be seen from the data below, among those with high knowledge there are 6 individuals with an age range of 18 to 30 years, one individual with an age range of 31 to 50 years, and three others with an age range of 51 to 70 years. Relating this to the total number of individuals in that age group, it is easy to see that between the ages of 51 and 70 the individuals have higher economic knowledge, in fact it is evident from the percentage of about 27% compared to about 9.50% in the first age group and 20% in the second age group.

In contrast, the largest number of people with average knowledge is concentrated in the 18-30 age group with a percentage of about 52 percent or 33 individuals out of the total of 63, again in this level between the ages of 31 and 50 about 40 percent or two individuals and between the 51 and 70 years old around 45% or 5 people. Finally, regarding poor knowledge there is about the same percentage of people in each age group{. Between the ages of 18 and 30 it is around 38%, between the ages of 31 and 50 around 40% and between 51 and 70 years around 27 percent.

The level of knowledge by age

Perception of risk by age							
	18-30 years	%	31-50 years	%	51-70 years	%	Total
High knowledge	6	10%	1	20%	3	27%	10
Average knowledge	33	52%	2	40%	5	45%	40
Poor knowledge	24	38%	2	40%	3	9%	29
						27%	
Total	63	100%	5	100%	11	100%	79

In conclusion, after analyzing economic knowledge I decided to break down and cross-reference this data with another variable analyzed earlier namely risk appetite.

To recapitulate, the risk-prone people are 26, those with moderate tolerance are 33, and 20 are risk-averse. This analysis resulted in the following values: risk-averse people with high knowledge are 5 or 6% of the total sample, 14 were found to be always risk-averse with, however, intermediate knowledge for a percentage value of about 18% and 7 with risk-averse and low knowledge for a value of about 9%. People with moderate tolerance toward risk are divided as follows: high knowledge 2.50% or 2 people, intermediate knowledge about 19% or 15 people and, poor knowledge 16 people as well as about 20%.

As for the risk-averse, it can be seen that 3 people possess high knowledge (3.80%), 12 people medium knowledge (about 15%) and 5 people poor knowledge (about 6%).

From this analysis it can be easily guessed that those with poor knowledge have a moderate tolerance for risk, this shows that those who hold insufficient financial knowledge are neither totally averse nor totally risk-averse.

People with average knowledge, on the other hand, have very similar values in all three categories of risk perception. This demonstrates that risk propensity or risk aversion does not depend so much on the knowledge of a person, but by the way they are influenced by circumstances and emotions, so it is subjective expectations that guide individuals in the choice process.

Level of knowledge and perception of risk

Level of knowledge and perception of risk						
	Risk-averse		Moderate tolerance		Risk aversion	Total
High knowledge	5	6.33%	2	3%	3	4%	10
Average knowledge	14	17.72%	15	19%	12	15%	41
Poor knowledge	7	8.86%	16	20%	5	6%	28
Total	26		33		20		79

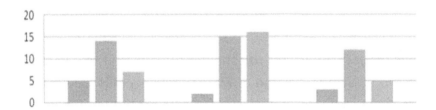

4.2 Detection of behavioral errors

The second part of the questionnaire consists of 16 questions each representing a different type of error in order to analyze and confirm all behavioral errors not only from a theoretical point of view, but also through empirical analysis. Especially, a check with the relevant literature will be carried out to conduct a comparison.

From this elaborate analysis, nine different errors could be developed and analyzed and more specifically the following: risk attitude, optimism, framing effect, mental accounting, loss aversion, disposition effect, fear of regret, instinct and shortcut thinking and finally dynamic inconsistency, myopia and procrastination.

These behaviors were studied by referring to one or more questions from the questionnaire, where based on the answers the sample gave, all the theories outlined in the previous chapters could be confirmed through empirical evidence.

These errors were examined individually through theoretical commentary and numerical demonstration by quantifying the subjects making them, to highlight the characteristics of the reference sample and go on to study the most frequent error among these treated.

However, it is important to consider the fact that this paper is based on a sample limited of 79 individuals composed mainly of college students and thus some results are influenced by variables such as age {and level of education.

In addition, the order in which these errors are represented does not follow the same order in which the questions included in the questionnaire are arranged, in order to create a logical thread between them and understand what connection there is between them.

4.2.1 Risk aptitude

The first question in the second part of the questionnaire is about respondents' attitude to risk, that is, how they turn out when they have to make a decision, unlike the previous question about risk appetite, which was based on personal preferences. It is asked, "Suppose you can invest 500 dollars in one company or you can split the money into five different companies{Which investment has more risk?" Subjects could choose whether the riskier investment was by investing the money in only one company, in five different companies or they could state that they were not aware of the solution.

The majority of the sample i.e. 91%, answered correctly, subjects are therefore aware that the risk is higher when deciding to invest in only one company. Only 9% stated that they were not aware of the answer, but none of the 79 respondents answered that the risk is greater when investing in five different companies.

Suppose you can invest 500 dollars in one company or you can Subdivide the money into 5 different companies. Which investment has greater risk?

Risk more if I invest in only one company	72	91%
Risk more if I invest in 5 different companies	0	0%
Don't know	7	9%
Total	79	100%

It is interesting to note that among those who stated that they did not know the answer to this question, that is, 7 out of 79 people or 9 percent are only individuals who hold medium and low knowledge, but none who hold high knowledge in business and finance. This is best demonstrated in the table below where we show that those with high knowledge answered correctly the 100%.

The justification for this lies in the fact that among the factors affecting attitude to risk is the level of knowledge as well as gender, age {and level of education. In fact, the data analysis shows that men have more attitude to risk as 88% or 30 men out of the total of 34, identified the riskiest investment while as for women 93% or 42 out of 45 women. With reference to age {it is interesting to note that in the age group between 18 and 30 years old 95 percent answered correctly, in the 31-50 age group 80 percent, and in the 51 and 70 years old 72 percent.

In reference to the level of knowledge, on the other hand, we note that all those with high knowledge answered correctly, among those holding medium knowledge 92 percent answered correctly, and among those who demonstrated low knowledge 86 percent answered correctly.

While when compared with educational level, among those who answered correctly, 85 percent hold a middle school degree or less, 98 percent a high school diploma, 50 percent a bachelor's degree, and another 40 percent a master's degree; the remaining people could not answer the question.

Risk aptitude thus represents the willingness to bear equity losses due to the failure of the financial instrument in which we have decided to invest. The more this propensity grows, the more willing we are to accept that our investments will not perform as expected. From this analysis, it appears that individuals are able to recognize risk, but in addition to the personal characteristics of the investor there are other elements that influence when deciding to invest and can negatively affect the decision making.

	I risk more if I invest in only one company		I risk more if I invest in 5 different companies		I don't know	
Gender	Responses	%			Responses	%
Female	42	93.00%	-	-	3	7%
Male	30	88.00%	-	-	4	12%
Total	72		-	-	7	
Age						
18-30 years	60	95%	-	-	3	5%
31-50 years	4	80%	-	-	1	20%
51-70 years	8	72%	-	-	3	28%
Total	72				7	
Knowledge						
High	10	100%	-	-	0	0%
Medium	37	92%	-	-	3	8%
Low	25	86%	-	-	4	14%
Total	72				7	
Education						
Junior high school or below	6	85%			1	15%
Diploma	62	98%			1	2%
Bachelor's degree	2	50%			2	50%
Master's degree	2	40%			3	60%
Total	72				7	

4.2.2 Optimism

One such factor that negatively influences decisions is optimism, a bias that was illustrated in the first chapter where it was pointed out that individuals may overestimate the chances of positive outcomes occurring, this in the financial sphere leads to fatal errors. The 79 subjects were asked whether investing today

100 dollars in the Italian stock market (in the Ftse Mib stocks) one year from now is it possible to make a gain or a loss to analyze the optimism among the sample. It turned out that 38% of the subjects believe it is possible to obtain a loss and 33% a gain.

In your opinion, investing 100 dollars in the Italian stock market today (in the stocks Ftse Mib, the most important index of the Milan stock exchange)

One year from now is it possible to make a gain or a loss?

Gain	26	33%
Loss	30	38%
I don't know	23	29%
Total	79	100%

It was also found that the most optimistic subjects are those in the age group of 31 to 50 years (40%) instead those who expect a loss are to be found in the age group of 18 to 30 years (44%). However, it should be kept in mind that the composition of the age groups 31 to 50 and 51 to 70 are numerically small compared to the much larger first age group.

[93]

As seen earlier in the first chapter, according to the studies conducted by Puri and Robinson it is possible to note that moderately confident individuals, i.e., those who answered "loss," are less risk-averse; in fact, among those who were identified as risk-averse, 45 percent believe that in a year's time there will be a loss because such individuals have a negative outlook and 30 percent a gain, while among those who were found to be risk-averse, 38 percent believe there will be a gain and 31 percent a loss. It is worth noting that individuals most often make biased predictions toward scenarios believed to be positive and that this generates a willingness to underwrite high-risk investments even when there is actually little appetite for risk.

There is no stability of preferences toward risk with respect to the way the problem is presented, thus we speak of the framing effect, previously illustrated that belies rationality in decision making.

	Age						Risk propensity					
	18-30 years		31-50 years		51-70 years		Perception of risk		Moderate tolerance		Risk-averse	
Gain	21	33%	2	40%	4	36%	10	38%	10	30%	6	30%
Loss	28	44%	0	0%	1	9%	8	31%	13	39%	9	45%
I don't know	14	22%	3	60%	6	55%	8	31%	10	30%	5	25%
Total	63	100%	5	100%	11	100%	26	100%	33	100%	20	100%

4.2.3 Framing effect

The framing effect is intended to describe the phenomenon by which subjects vary their preferences depending on how the problem is presented. To test this effect, respondents were asked the question formulated by Kahneman and Tversky in which they were presented with a situation in which they had to cope with a rare disease that predicted 600 people would die. Program A predicted that 200 people would be saved, while Program B predicted that with a 1/3 probability 600 people would be saved and with 2/3 no one would be saved.

Approximately 70% of the 79 respondents choose program A i.e. saving 200 people, as verified by the two scholars. In a second step they are asked to choose between letting 400 people die (program C) or no one dies with probability 1/3 or 600 people die with probability 2/3 (program D). In this case 54% of the subjects chose the second alternative while about 45% chose to have 400 people die. Actually, on reflection for a moment, it can be seen that the alternative which plans to have 400 people die and the one in which it is decided to have 200 survive are identical, as are the other two in that they induce different frames due to different formulation.

When confronted with the first question, subjects coded the lives of the rescued people as the gains and thus are risk-averse in having to choose between A and B, whereas when asked the second question individuals associate death with losses placing themselves risk-averse in having to decide between C and D. By means of a simple calculation it is easy to see how all four alternatives yield an identical result i.e., they save themselves 200 people. To have failed to notice this equality is to have fallen into the trap of the framing effect. This process causes the subjects to whom the question is put to accept it as it is and do not try to streetcar it with alternative words, in fact we are not able to contextualize the problem but on the contrary we segregate it. Instead of considering all the pros and cons of the decision to be made we act too immediately.

Which vaccination program do you choose to fight an epidemic			And between these other two programs		
600 people will be saved with a 1/3 probability but may happen that no one will be saved with a 2/3 probability	24	30%	No one dies with a probability of 1/3 but may happen that all 600 die with a probability of 2/3	43	54%
200 people are saved	55	70%	400 people die	36	46%
Total	79	100%	Total	79	100%

Interestingly, among those who gave an incorrect answer to the question, more women 58% than men 50%, and thus the latter were more rational at the choice stage. The framing effect is evidence that cognitive biases lead our brains to make judgments and evaluations based on intuition and contrary to logic. It is important to remember how these effects are related to loss aversion and mental accounting, which was discussed in reference to the development of prospect theory.

	Female		Male	
600 people will be saved with a 1/3 probability but may happen that no one will be saved with a 2/3 probability	13	29%	11	32%
200 people are saved	32	71%	23	68%
Total	45	100%	34	100%
No one dies with a probability of 1/3 but may happen that all 600 die with a probability of 2/3	26	58%	17	50%
400 people die	19	42%	17	50%
Total	45	100%	34	100%

4.2.4 Mental accounting

To analyze how mental accounting acts among subjects, respondents were asked to decide how they would spend their money, primarily that from 1,000 dollar lottery winnings. Forty-one percent of the sample said that that money would go to increase their bank or postal deposit. According to behavioral finance, extraordinary income is more easily spent than ordinary income; in fact, respondents turn out to be savers.

This may find justification when one considers the fact that most of the sample consists of young individuals who prefer to deposit money rather than invest it in securities or spend it on the purchase of durable goods. Twenty-three percent said they would invest the money in a retirement fund, 19 percent in the purchase of durable goods, and 13% to buy stocks and bonds.

This question was submitted in order to test the mental accounting theory that individuals seem to use to create an ideal portfolio. They make their decisions by following a kind of pyramid of needs, starting with security needs and then continuing with increasingly ambitious and income needs.

Subjects were then asked how they would use the money from an increase in monthly income; 32 percent say they would spend that money to buy durable goods, 28 percent would increase their deposits, 19 percent would buy stocks, and 18 percent would invest in retirement funds. It is possible to see how the sample is distributed in more or less equally among all possible alternatives, in fact each individual chooses how to invest his or her money based on what he or she considers most necessary.

Although as a consequence of a monthly increase in income, individuals are more likely to purchase durable goods since it is a matter of satisfying secure needs by possessing the security of a certain income.

	Suppose you won $1,000 in the lottery, how would you be willing to employ the entire winnings?		Suppose that thanks to a career advancement your monthly income has increased by $1,000. how would you be willing to employ your new income?	
	Responses	%	Responses	%
Buying stocks/bonds	10	13%	15	19%
Purchasing durable goods	15	19%	25	32%
Increasing your deposit in the bank / post office	32	41%	22	28%
Investing in a retirement fund	18	23%	14	18%
I don't know	4	5%	3	4%
Total	79	100%	79	100%

4.2.5 Loss aversion

As previously defined subjects are much more sensitive to losses rather than gains, it was explained in the second chapter more precisely in the prospect theory, that in the domain of losses individuals are more risk-averse while in the area of gains they are more risk-averse. Demonstrating this, one of the questions in the questionnaire gave respondents a choice between two alternatives, "Lose an amount equal to 200 with a 50% probability or lose an amount equal to 0 with a 50% probability" or "Lose an amount equal to 100"; 57% preferred the first alternative i.e., the riskier one, while 43% chose the second option.

Whereas when asked the same question but referring to gains, then at the time when they had to choose between: "Earn an amount equal to 200 with a 50% probability or earn an amount equal to 0 with a 50% probability" or "Earn an amount equal to 100" the majority chose the safer alternative (57%) instead the remaining subjects the first solution (43%).

From these results, we can confirm Kahneman and Tversky's theory that states that individuals tend to consider a loss to a greater extent than a gain of the same amount; in fact, in our particular case, about 6 out of 10 subjects opted for a sure gain instead only 4 out of 10 opted for a certain loss.

What would you prefer if you had to choose between the probability of:			What would you prefer if you had to choose between the:		
	Responses	%		Responses	%
Losing an amount equal to 200 with a 50% probability or losing an amount equal to 0 with a 50% probability	45	57%	Earning an amount equal to 200 with a 50% probability or earning an amount equal to 0 with a 50% probability	34	43%
Lose an amount equal to 100	34	43%	Earning an amount equal to 100	45	57%
Total	79	100%		79	100%

4.2.6 Disposition effect

How gains and losses are treated is related to the disposition effect, by which investors avoid the fear of regret. To understand how we behave when a stock appreciates or depreciates, it was decided to ask respondents two questions. The first says, "Imagine you bought a stock at 60 dollars. In the last month, the price rises to 120 dollars. In the absence of new specific information about the stock, how do you act? " (Consob); subjects had to choose whether to buy that stock again, do nothing, sell some of it, or sell all of it.

When the price of a security in the portfolio rises, usually the investor decides to sell it even if the outlook has remained unchanged. In fact, the 38% of the 79 respondents said they would sell some of it and 35% would sell all of it. In contrast, 19% were neutral and decided not to make any transactions, and only 8% would buy more.

The second question asked, "Imagine you bought a stock at 60 dollars. In the last month the price drops to 30 dollars. In the absence of any new specific information about the stock, how do you behave?" in this case a loss has developed, so the investor is generally willing to keep the stock in his or her portfolio, although he or she would not buy it again.

In fact, analyzing the data showed that as many as 61 percent of respondents said they would do nothing in a situation of depreciating securities, while 20 percent said they would buy more and only 10 percent would sell some and 9 percent would sell all. Investors, have a hard time recognizing their losses and thus tend to keep "losing" securities in their portfolios for too long, while selling "winning" ones immediately to anticipate monetary gratification.

In a situation such as the one just described, selling the security would be to give birth to the mistake, so by delaying the sale, the fear of regret arising from the possibility of the security's appreciation is also translated. Even winning stocks still contain the possibility of regret, in case the price falls before we succeed in selling the stock.

Imagine you purchased a stock at $60. in the last month, the price rises to $120. In the absence of new specific information about the stock, how do you act?			Imagine you bought a stock at $60. in the last month, the price drops to 30. In the absence of new specific information about the stock, how do you act?		
	Responses	%		Responses	%
I will buy more	6	8%	I will buy more	16	20%
I will do nothing	15	19%	I will do nothing	48	61%
I will sell part of it	30	38%	I will sell part of it	8	10%
I will sell all of it	28	35%	I will sell all of it	7	9%
Total	79	100%	Total	79	100%

4.2.7 Fear of regret

On a daily basis, subjects try to avoid feeling regrets in fact it could be seen that these people deposit money in the current account rather than invest it. As many as 48 out of 79 respondents say they deposit savings only in the checking account, while 21 are those who in addition to depositing money also decided to invest it, as well as about a quarter of the total.

Individuals who decide to make investments usually seek to anticipate the displeasure they would feel if their choices turn out to be wrong. For this reason, irrational behaviors such as immobility are triggered, i.e., we have seen how as many as 61 percent of respondents at the time the stock price falls prefer not to make decisions to avoid falling into error. Then there is imitation of others' behaviors, somewhat to share responsibility with other individuals or even to attribute it to others.

In order to analyze how much individuals are affected by the attitudes of others, it was decided to include three questions in the questionnaire: "How much do you agree with these statements: the majority is always right, before choosing an investment I look at what others do and do things I later regret" (Consob). Subjects responded according to a scale of 1 to 5 based on how much they agreed with these statements.

As can be seen from the results obtained in the first question "The majority has always right," 35 percent of individuals responded that they agreed, fairly and very agreement. On the next question, however, "I do things that I later regret," individuals agreeing with this statement increased by 5 percent. Since these two questions were not investment-specific, they failed to fully confirm to us how the error of regret is generated.

This confirmation, however, came with the more specific question regarding namely "Before choosing an investment what do others do" where most, about 6 out of 10 individuals said that they agreed with following the behaviors of others, in fact individuals are inclined to imitate others to avoid regret, in this case we speak of herd effect.

Subjects prefer to follow others' decisions rather than make independent choices, but hardly when following the crowd do decisions turn out to be right. This is a type of decision-making error that also results from the use of heuristics, as there is a tendency to oversimplify processes by creating incorrect solutions.

How much do you agree with these statements from 1 to 5, where 1 indicates "Not at all agree" to 5 "Very much agree"? - The majority is always right			How much do you agree with these statements from 1 to 5, where 1 indicates "Not at all agree" to 5 "Very much agree"? - Before choosing an investment I look at what others are doing		How much do you agree with these statements from 1 to 5, where 1 indicates "Not at all agree" to 5 "Very much agree"? - I do things that I seductively regret	
	Responds	%	Responds	%	Responds	%
1	24	30%	19	24%	14	18%
2	27	35%	16	20%	33	42%
3	20	25%	28	36%	19	24%
4	7	9%	13	16%	10	12%
5	1	1%	3	4%	3	4%
Total	79	100%	79	100%	79	100

4.2.8 Instinct and thinking shortcuts

Much of individuals' choices are made instinctively and through shortcuts in thinking; in fact, to analyze how subjects are influenced by such heuristic behaviors, this question was proposed to the sample: "A bat and a ball cost 1.10 dollars. The bat costs 1 dollar more than the ball. How much does the ball cost?" Respondents could choose from three alternatives: 10 cents, 5 cents or they could abstain by stating that they did not know the answer.

This question is part of a test carried out by Frederik (2005) who proposed three questions, including this one, to students at the most prestigious American universities noting that the solution that was given by the respondents was most often wrong. In fact, it was possible to verify this theory of his as 51 percent of the respondents to this questionnaire gave an incorrect solution, namely that the cost of the ball equals 10 cents, but if the ball cost 10 cents the bat would cost 1.10 dollars and their sum would be 1.20 dollars.

Thus, the correct answer is 5 cents, but only 32 out of 79 subjects answered exactly. In fact, those who are asked questions of this type are inclined to answer using the first intuition that arises in their minds, without using the necessary resources they have available to analyze the question. Thus, it can be guessed how these individuals are inclined to be irrational, a behavior that then spills over into financial choices as well. They use mental shortcuts, the so-called heuristics discussed in the first chapter, to be able to simplify the problem by facilitating the decision, in reality all this generates errors of perception. Reasoning by stereotypes does not always lead to the most optimal solution especially when it comes to investments, in which it is necessary to assess the risk and analyze the available data.

A bat and a ball together cost one dollar and 10 cents. The bat costs one dollar more than the ball. How much does the ball cost?

10 cents	40	51%
5 cents	32	41%
I don't know	7	9%
Total	79	100%

4.2.9 Dynamic inconsistency, myopia and procrastination

An individual investor's choices most often are implemented through irrational or even illogical behavior. It may be the case that the same choice shifted to different time periods leads individuals to make opposite decisions, as can be seen in fact from the question in the questionnaire that asks respondents, "If you are offered 100 dollars today or 150 in a month what do you choose? ".

30% chose 100 dollars today while 70% preferred 150 dollars in one month. The same question postponed for six months and thus, "If you were offered 100 dollars in six months and 150 dollars in seven months?" generated different results, 12% more than in the previous question preferred to wait for a higher return so they chose 150 dollars in seven months.

It can be seen that between the two answers, 100 dollars or 150 dollars, the difference in return coincided with the same waiting time in both questions i.e. one month, however more individuals in the first question preferred to have an immediate gain (30%) than in the second where only 18% chose the more instantaneous option.

This amount of individuals maintained an illogical behavior in that they changed their preferences despite the fact that the conditions of the question remained the same, i.e., the same time frame and the same gain.

If you are offered 100 today or 150 in a month what do you choose?			What if you were offered 100 in six months and 150 in seven months?		
	Responds	%		Responds	%
150 in a month	55	70%	150 in 7 months	65%	82%
100 now	24	30%	100 in 6 months	14%	18%
Total	79	100%	Total	79%	100%

4.3 Final considerations on the empirical work

From this chapter it is possible to draw some conclusions, although not definitive, but which are in agreement with the main reference literature.

This study made it possible to compare the theories presented in the previous chapters with a sample of individuals and verify the correctness of all these theses. Assuming that this is a limited sample consisting mainly of young individuals, as well as students, it could be seen that the level of financial education turns out to be medium-low, as well as the risk appetite of the respondents is placed in a medium tolerance level, with reference to the questions chosen specifically to derive this information.

Regarding the second part of the questionnaire, that is, the part referring to the detection of behavioral errors, it could be seen that most of the subjects make mistakes. In particular, some of these errors are more frequent than others, and some affect the female gender more than the male gender.

The sample turns out to be able to recognize risk i.e., unwilling to suffer asset losses, however, it is possible for them to make biased predictions and underwrite risky investments when in fact they are risk-averse. This happens from the moment stability in the choice process is lacking, due to the way the problem is exposed. It could be seen that one of the questions that misled the sample the most was precisely the question about the framing effect. The question that was asked presupposed logical reasoning by which to maintain the same criterion of choice, actually as illustrated above, when subjects are in the area of gains they are more risk-averse, while when they are in the domain of losses they are risk-averse.

Mental accounting theory was then tested, where it is evident that subjects are savers, in that most of them prefer to deposit money in their bank or postal account, while as a consequence of an increase in fixed income they prefer to purchase durable goods to satisfy another type of need because individuals decide how to invest money based on a pyramid of needs.

Respondents are thus more likely to deposit money rather than invest it, but those who decide to make investments develop irrational behaviors such as immobility and imitation of others' behaviors to have no responsibility and consequently avoid possible regrets. In fact, a significant percentage of subjects said they agreed with the statement "Before choosing an investment I look at what others are doing."

This type of error results from the use of heuristics that simplify processes by generating solutions that most often turn out to be wrong. People are negatively influenced by thinking shortcuts and usually make decisions by instinct, but reasoning by stereotypes generates errors of perception.

In fact, it was possible to see that a certain amount of individuals maintained illogical behavior by varying preferences even though the prospects of gain remained the same.

It is noteworthy, then, that the sample is generally averse to losses, as these are considered more significant than gains even if they are of equal amounts.

From this chapter, finally, it can be seen, how the sample is overall predisposed to making behavioral errors, especially those concerning the framing effect and loss aversion, where subjects were most misled by the questions that were precisely intended to draw useful information to infer how involved individuals are.

Conclusion

The paper was created with the intention of analyzing how the individual investor behaves, which is why it was chosen to present the different factors that affect the decision-making process, so as to outline the likely figure of the investor.

It could be seen that empirical evidence shows that no individual exhibits the characteristics of perfect rationality and welfare maximization, principles supported instead by traditional finance.

In reality, each individual has different characteristics because they are influenced by different moods, individual goals or contexts surrounding them. For this reason, behavioral finance has repeatedly pointed out that individuals are subject to cognitive errors as well as behavioral biases.

This paper lays out, in support of the claims made by finance behavioral, key heuristics and a range of cognitive and emotional errors and preferences. In fact, it was found by studying empirical examples directly formulated by scholars that indeed individuals turn out to be influenced by factors that cause them to err and lead them to behavioral anomalies, as was also subsequently noted by the empirical study carried out in person. Obviously, these errors gain significance when made by investors, as a wrong investment can damage his economic and financial situation.

Next, in the Italian economic environment, the characteristics of the investor were outlined, who is very keen on saving by seeking investments that express security and are short-term. In addition, special attention was given to managed savings as the investor due to insufficient financial skills does not sufficiently diversify the portfolio, in fact he relies on third parties to manage savings. Particular emphasis was then placed on asset management and its component instruments.

More specifically, the main work was conducted in order to test the practical relevance of behavioral errors, to understand how subjects react when faced with investment choices, and to test the theories reported in the first chapters.

It has been ascertained how indeed decisions are influenced by a variety of both cognitive and emotional factors. In addition, financial education is believed to be a preponderant part of the decision-making stage; in fact, most of the subjects interviewed possesses average or low knowledge that therefore hinders their understanding of the questions to which they were submitted.

However, subjects with high knowledge are not to be excluded because it has been shown how they also incur and fall victim to bias in decision making. Thus, it can be stated how irrationality in the choice stage is not only influenced by financial education but that there are also possible correlations with other factors such as mental shortcuts. It has been verified that subjects reason instinctively but make mistakes as they process information too simplistically.

Another deviation of the logical process of choice was the perception and evaluation of risk, as this was based on how subjects perceived gains or losses and mainly turn out to be averse to the latter.

It was then confirmed how the importance given to gains rather than losses is related to the disposition effect by which individuals avoid regret, in fact they prefer to deposit money rather than invest it. If they decide to invest instead, they follow the behaviors of others rather than making autonomous choices.

Currently being aware and being aware that behavioral mistakes could be made can lead individuals to change such behaviors perhaps by increasing financial knowledge or deciding to consult a professional. It is believed that money should be managed effectively and that lack of knowledge or fear of making mistakes should not generate investment limitations, but rather create an opportunity in which to realize that financial advice confers benefits both from the perspective of performance and portfolio diversification. In fact, the choice to analyze the situation of the Italian investor gives the possibility to reflect and deepen these issues going to increase the awareness inherent in each subject.

PART II

Chatting about finance, ethics and philosophy.

Let's start with an example. In December 1991 Lawrence Summers in a memorandum says the World Bank should encourage the migration of polluting industries to developing countries. So let's clean our own house, stop doing polluting processing such as plastics, fertilizers, etc., and have developing countries do it. As an economist he finds reasons that also seem very valid:

1. If pollution is bad for health, the costs of health loss depend on the incomes to which those who die or get sick give up. So is it better for a person who earns $10 a day to get sick or the person in New York who earns $1,000 a day? If the one who earns $1,000 a day loses one day of work, it is the same as if the one who earns 10 lost 100 days of work. So if we had the ability to measure the health damage created by pollution, we should move polluting industries to places where people are poorest, that is, to the country with the lowest wages and where people have trouble finding work. That way we give them jobs, and even if the productions are somewhat polluting, economically the harm produced to these people is less economically impactful than the harm you would produce in another place. We don't like that reasoning very much, but Lawrence Summers says it's the same thing we do when we don't want to do certain things, so we pay someone, who maybe has less choice than we do, to do them.

2. The cost of pollution may not be linear, so the cost is very low in the beginning. In an unpolluted country, the first doses of pollution weigh less than the later doses, so an already industrialized country like the United States or Germany is better off exchanging the same dose of pollution with a less polluted country. The sixteenth hour is work is heavier than the sixth hour so the super busy may be willing to pay the not-so-busy to be replaced.

3. Finally, the demand for a clean environment also has aesthetic reasons. Some economist observes that sensitivity to pollution increases with the level of wealth of economic systems, so when an economic system becomes wealthy and people more affluent, they are more interested in having a manicured park, not having the smokestack smoking in the background, having less traffic on the street, etc. So there is also an aspect of pleasantness, not only related to health but there is an aesthetic aspect. There is a principle that if you remember is Ricardo's opportunity cost, that is, it agrees that the work should be done by the most suitable people. He gives the example of the lawyer and the secretary, he said that the lawyer in deciding whether to write a letter or dictate it to the secretary, should not look at whether he is better than the secretary but he should look at how much it costs to pay the secretary and how much he earns in the time it does not take him to write the letter. This is the theory of comparative advantage, which mind you is already there in the world. Because if we take the example of Milan (Italy) , there is a street called via Orti because several decades ago there were vegetable gardens. Later they found out that making houses or offices out of them made more money so it's not that people stopped eating salad, they simply told people

who lived in places outside of Milan you grow the salad and then bring it to Milan because the value you get from putting that piece of land to another use is greater. But then it's like pollution, we move pollution to develop countries, however, we don't like it.

All our reasoning in this course will be based on just this kind of reasoning. There are things that seem rational and that are, that have perfect economic logic like this reasoning, however, they create some fatigue in our minds. Whenever we choose, that has ethical implications. So we start making a distinction, we have an aspect that is called "positive" which is Summers, if I take a polluting industry and move it to a developing country I save money, if oranges instead of having the CEO of a bank pick them I have an undocumented immigrant pick them, I save a lot of money. It's not that the CEO of the bank is not capable of picking oranges, but it doesn't pay off. So positive economics simply tells us that certain things are convenient.

Then there are regulatory aspects, that is, what you have to do, what is right to do. From a positive point of view, if oranges are picked by an illegal immigrant I can sell them for $1 for 2 pounds, if a company executive picked them and I had to pay him the salary he gets for being an executive then those oranges would cost $10 for 2 pounds as a consequence of the fact that the labor cost is much higher.

So if you pollute in the U.S. and therefore you have to reduce pollution, take the case of steel factories, it's not that you can't reduce the pollution that a steel mill produces, simply what a certain number of billions. If you spend those billions, then the steel costs much more, and in that case, I don't sell anymore because ships come from China with steel at a lower price. And then from a positive point of view, it is all clear, from a regulatory point of view you have to see what is right to do.

So we will have to develop evaluation criteria for these things. For example, what assumptions is this letter based on? They are assumptions that we do not see right away because we are used to this way of reasoning, however this way of reasoning we have to realize that it is a way of reasoning, that is, we are completely immersed in a culture that is not necessarily the only culture that exists. The example that is given in these cases is if you go and get the Code of Hammurabi, it says some crazy things that are not acceptable now.

And this code was the pinnacle of civilization at that time. So the first thing we say about Lawrence Summers is that he is making an account based on money, but this is not a natural law like the law of gravity, from a historical point of view it is the same thing as the Code of Hammurabi. So the rules that govern the world right now are historical rules anyway, and if we want to analyze them we have to start from the assumption that they are in themselves as right or wrong as those that governed the world in Hammurabi's time.

But you can go even closer to us, and we will see this by talking about Aristotle, all the ancient philosophers thought that slavery was a normal thing. Aristotle actually wrote parts where he says that because slave labor exists, slaves must exist. And Aristotle was one of the greatest thinkers of antiquity.

So making an economic comparison to us today is very convincing, we have to see the cost-benefit analysis. It's not clear but from what I've studied if we had done the cost-benefit analysis on the pyramids. One builds the pyramid for other reasons, not for cost-benefit analysis.

So today the convention of saying things are done if it's convenient, and Summers tells us this, to us convinces, but it's not necessarily the only way of reasoning, because for many cultures and for many centuries past this was not the only way of reasoning.

So many works of antiquity certainly were not done on the basis of cost-benefit analysis. Yuval Noah Harari's book "Sapiens. From Animals to Gods" tells why man has become so haunting in the world, i.e., mankind has developed a lot compared to other animal forms. There are biological reasons, but mainly because man is a social animal and to keep very large groups together he creates abstract myths.

These abstract myths are used to create large communities so the pyramids could be a way to visualize myths and make the poor peasants work near the Nile, and pay taxes, then someone with those taxes makes the pyramids but they don't make them throw money away, they make them because the myth is part of the social cohesion that makes that civilization possible. But then is capitalism a myth? It may well be.

So when we want to judge whether something is ethical or not we must first ask ourselves but where does this idea come from, the fact that he says the cost of producing these things in one place is lower than in another so it is convenient to move production means that he as a decision rule uses the comparison of money, which is one way of representing reality, but historically it is not necessarily the only way. It is a very common way now because the history of humanity sharing one way of thinking is very recent.

So as first thing capitalism is a convention, we have to start from the reference context which is not necessarily the only one. So when he proposes this, he is implicitly saying dear my interlocutors about capitalism there is no discussion, we think the same way, that is, the criterion for judging whether something is done or not is just to compare different utilities. The second thing, it doesn't take into consideration what we said at the beginning, that is this thing maybe convinces us however a little bit disturbs us, someone might say it doesn't seem very fair to me that someone else has to get sick so that I don't get sick, in the end, if I have to choose it will be so but I don't like it very much.

This kind of reasoning does not take it into consideration, so it does not take emotions into consideration. An additional factor, this reasoning only takes into consideration people, not cultures, basically we are simply saying that it is better for a poor person to get sick than for a rich person to get sick, it is better for a poor person to do a bad job than for a rich person to do a bad job: comparison of subjects. Be careful, though, because moving a polluting industry to a certain country could affect other things as well, for example, the culture of that country.

It is well known that with industrialization the culture of people changes a lot. One very obvious thing is that if women work they have fewer children. It involves great social impacts to move a product from one point to another, it can also involve cultural changes, it can change the ways of living, of relating, all these things are not talked about. These are some of the things to consider, the so-called framework, which is the convention on which an argument is based, and you always have to be very open about that. The broader consequences, so not just on individuals, are all important things.

This reasoning has been the subject of much analysis so there are articles etc. I will give you a brief summary of the other elements that can be considered.

1. What criterion is used? We said it before, capitalist criterion, but does the results or the process matter in this area? As we will see sometimes process matters a lot in decisions, i.e. if a fellow citizen of mine comes and takes money from me it is theft, if I don't pay taxes which is the same thing it is also theft. The difference is that because I voted or can vote anyway, the state that imposes taxation does so with my consent, so in a world, without a state, if someone comes along and takes money from me to use him I don't like it, would call it theft. In a world where there is a state, if I don't pay taxes I am treated as someone who steals, so the opposite. The difference is in the system within which the action takes place, so the results count but the process also counts.

2. Which method of evaluation do we use? A single method as Summers does or multiple methods, do we consider multiple aspects?

So for example also the ethical, aesthetic aspects, etc. In other words, is it possible to put a price on anything? Summers gives a list of examples. There are some things you can pay to do or not do, such as uterus for hire. If we use only affordability as a method of evaluation, certainly there will be some young girl in full health and unemployed, who for $20,000 can also do it. However, not everyone is persuaded by such reasoning.

So the economic convenience is clear, because with the money Kim Kardashian does not lose because of the damage to her body, she rents another girl's uterus and therefore both of them gain, however, if we limit the reasoning from an economic point of view. If they tell us that, to someone something doesn't add up.

Another example, in California there is a lot of traffic so they made reserved lanes for carpooling: if you are in a car with at least 2 other people, you can go in those lanes. Those lanes are less crowded and you arrive earlier. It's a good principle, because we reduce pollution that way. After a short time, however, California said, if one is alone and gives me $5 he can still go. So is the principle important or is the money important? Obviously the person who made this proposal tells you, with all the money I make then I can make new highways, new pollution standards, etc.

Same concept is Area C in Milan, so you don't have to pollute, but if you pay a little you can. I put a little disincentive. The best known Summers case, about whether it matters more principle or consequence, is the walrus case. Some countries banned walrus hunting because it was becoming extinct. The American hunters feel a little bad about it, however, some native Eskimo communities say this ruins our culture, because for us walrus hunting is an important thing in our culture, we used to make lamp oil with the fat, we used to make fur with the skin, we used to eat the meat, etc.

So to preserve the culture it was said each household has the right to kill one walrus per year. After that you know Americans are businessmen, an agency pops up and puts up a whole thing whereby the Eskimo goes with the Texan gentleman to hunt and the Eskimo takes the walrus away.

So everyone is happy because the Eskimo gets the walrus and $500 for the trouble, the American is happy because for a time he could not hunt the walrus and he comes back to it. The walrus is always the same, he was not happy before and he is not happy after. Who is sad in all this? A little bit the princes, we are a little bit disturbed by this.

This means the speech we started from, that sometimes the comparison of economic reasoning alone does not tell us everything, sometimes we feel that something is missing.

And so not everything can be bought, although apparently everyone is happy. In the surrogate uterus, even the child might be happy because instead of being tossed up and down in cabs while in the womb, he's sitting at home quietly with little noise, balanced diet, no smoking, no drugs, he's happy too. Nobody's loss but the principle doesn't add up. So where is the mistake? The error, the thing to question, is the criterion we use, if we only compare the utility of individuals, we may lose a piece of it.

3. What criteria should we use? Then one thing is the framework, the context, the way of examining. We said today's world examines things from a purely economic point of view. Once you set up this system, this language what criterion do you use? You could use for example the criterion of freedom, and we will see, that it means all people are only free, for example, taxation with the criterion of freedom doesn't work much because if I am free the money is mine.

So much so that in the United States there are minimal state theorists: from the state I don't want anything, I defend myself, I don't need the police because I shoot, I don't need the school because I teach my children what I want. I need some justice and I need somebody to run the military and that's it because then I also buy my own health care.

So there are some people who say anything more, it hinders my freedom. I want to live on my ranch with my horses, and my rifle and I'm doing just fine on my own. I don't want any interference from the state because that limits my freedom. There are philosophers as well as social and political groups who think this way. So the criterion to use when I have to judge whether something is right or wrong is the criterion of freedom, does it increase or reduce freedom?

Taxation is wrong because it reduces my freedom. Theft is wrong because it reduces my freedom. But there could be, for example, a criterion of utility, which is the one most commonly used, that does not go along with the criterion of freedom.

According to the criterion of utility you have to do what is most convenient. If it is more convenient to let one person die than to let 1,000 people die, according to the criterion of utility you have to choose to let one person die. Take for example the Twin Towers case, imagine in that case there was a terrorist suspect and the police knew that he knew certain things the day before, if we torture him and find out certain things, we save crazy consequences if we can avoid that thing.

So under the criterion of utility, it is clear, that you torture one person even if it is not right, but you compare the pain of one person with the benefit of thousands of other people. Under the criterion of freedom, you cannot compare the value of one life with the value of another.

Then there could be a criterion of justice, for example in the U.S. Constitution there is the principle of "life, liberty and the pursuit of happiness" so every American citizen has a right to his life, liberty, and the pursuit of happiness. It is the duty of the Republic to remove obstacles which, by limiting the liberty and equality of citizens, prevent the full development of the human person." The problem is that we like two things that are difficult to reconcile, freedom and equality because to be equal we have to be not completely free. For example, if we are in a society that rewards speed in running: whoever comes first gets money and the others get nothing.

At that point what happens is that the fastest person wins. It is not an egalitarian society because the one who is faster gets a lot, and the one who is less fast gets nothing. To make this society egalitarian is not that you can make the one who is slow go faster. The only way to make people more equal is to make the strongest a little less free.

And in fact, the libertarian political views, for example in the United States, are very radical as far as equality is concerned, that is, they answer you if you are born into an unfortunate social condition it's your problem, it's not me who has to help solve your problems, I have no merit to have been born the way I was born but I have no fault either. But that makes society less egalitarian. Do you want a very egalitarian society? The Soviet Union, Communist China, Cambodia. In Cambodia, during the Cultural Revolution, they killed people who wore glasses because they said intellectuals had advantages.

Since you cannot make those who have not studied know as much as those who have studied, how do you quickly eliminate inequality? You pull down those who have studied, and you reduce freedom to zero, as in totalitarian states. So the Constitution that talks about freedom and equality as if they were natural things, actually serve to hold differences together. Many social historians believe that a lot of the work that is done by political and social systems is like a huge lintel that is used to hold these huge contradictions together, that is, to make sure that people who believe that equality is a right thing but who also want to be free don't spend their time beating each other over the head, that is, they manage to have the principles of equality and freedom coexisting in the same society. Because if I want equality I can't have freedom, if I want freedom equality goes to hell. By the way, some people think that a lot of the social tensions of this last period stem from the liberalism of the 1980s.

So the criterion we use is not without economic consequences, and it is a cultural criterion. So what society should achieve, what rules we give ourselves, and are right or wrong has a lot to do with the conventions we use. Some American thinker says it's so true all that even school is a way to spread those social conventions that hold up inequality, the ruling class, etc. because in school you are taught a set of values that are not taken for granted, they are acquired, so one might say it's not a school but it's indoctrination, so much so that in some political systems in the past school was used for indoctrination.

So someone says things start very far upstream, it is a system of social control that allows certain rules to be decided. The one who decides the rules certainly is not the immigrants but it is the one who is in a position to decide at that time, and how will he decide them? We have to assume in his interest. And since those in a position to decide are usually also the strongest, it may be that they are somehow interested in preserving the inequalities that suit them.

So be careful because the architecture of our reasoning is important, it should not be taken for granted. So the criteria can be different and conflicting, for example, freedom and equality are difficult to reconcile.

Ethics is a reflection of people's behavior. In the field of economics and in the field of finance, many times we ask whether a behavior is ethical. There are some behaviors that are even illegal, such as insider trading, false accounting, and obstruction of supervision. The values of the banking committee of the past legislature and those that will begin to contain a lot of criticism of the behavior of bankers, banks, the SEC, auditing firms, etc. criticism of behavior and so they are ethical evaluations. When you say one did wrong or behaved badly, some things can be sanctioned by some law, but some things can also be misjudged from an ethical point of view. So ethics is understanding how we judge behavior, and in finance, there is a mountain of ethical judgments.

After that in addition to this vocabulary definition, there are other specifications, such as descriptive ethics. Descriptive ethics means to describe an ethical system. Socrates' ethics, I describe what he thought was right and wrong. In Socrates' ethics, there is the fact that slavery is right. In modern ethics, it is not. So with descriptive ethics, I describe an ethical system. We wouldn't like Hammurabi's ethics today, but it was an ethical system. Instead, normative ethics tells us how we should behave, for example, many companies have what is called a "code of ethics," a very simple code of ethics is Johnson&Johnson, which contains a set of principles, and the things they believe in. Normative ethics, that is, I say this is how I behave. Similar to that is applied ethics, which is how I behaved in certain cases, and how I apply ethical concepts to concrete cases. What is different, which we will not do, is the so-called "metaethics," which tells us where ethical principles come from. According to some they come from God, they may come from social conventions, from biological inclinations, so metaethics asks what is the origin of ethics, why did certain ethics develop? According to Harari it simply comes from the biological development of people. Basically, at some point man discovered agriculture, but according to him it may have even happened the other way around, that agriculture discovered man. In what sense? In the sense that someone from the tribes of gatherers and hunters discovered wheat, wheat is a highly weedy plant, because it allows you to get a lot of calories, once people discovered how to reproduce wheat, it's as if wheat found someone who spread it around the world. In fact, that's what happened because wheat comes from Asia Minor and now it's everywhere in the world. Once you do this thing, you lose the ability to do other things. In particular, the number of people there is now in the world is not compatible with a society of gatherers and hunters, because there are too many of us, we can only live by agriculture, industrialization, etc. Once you have that many, you have to find a way not to split up. If you put unsocialized people on the subway at 8 a.m., they would have a hard time not feeling attacked. Only social conventions allow us to collaborate with so many people to produce goods that sustain so many people, i.e. what Harari is saying is: you can't go back. From the agricultural revolution or the domestication of animals, there is no turning back. So ethics could come from that as well, because only with ethical principles can we cooperate in so many, only if we follow rules that we share without needing to discuss so much can we live in such complicated societies because they are so dense. It doesn't have much to do with the ethics of finance, but this also helps us to know that we have to look at things with a certain detachment: ethical systems are not stable, they last a long time but they are not stable. So much so that for a long time there was Socratic ethics, then for a long time there was scholastic ethics based on the fact that until the French Revolution a society dominated in which great weight was given to religion, in the sense that it was believed that power to the emperor came from God, etc. so religion had a much greater influence on society than it does now, then with the French Revolution and the Enlightenment this changed. So ethical systems change, slowly but they change, sometimes slowly but with interesting historical junctures. About the same time as the Enlightenment something happened that is very little known, the Lisbon earthquake. The Lisbon earthquake happened during the Enlightenment and it challenged the dominant thinking, which was does God exist? God is good, so he cannot do things too wrong. The Lisbon earthquake was exploited by the Enlightenment to challenge that. The cultural crisis was that practically the only neighborhood spared was the neighborhood in Lisbon where the houses of toleration were. Voltaire in particular, an Enlightenment philosopher, had made a big philosophical controversy about the fact that in the order provided by scholastic philosophy such a thing could not happen. So the problem of metaethics exists, it is not a given that the principles we see now are true forever, we always have to see where they come from, sometimes they are conventions.

Where does ethics have an impact, and why do we care about ethics? Because in the economic field there are some things on which ethics has little impact, for example on forecasting it has no impact. Economic policy and regulation, on the other hand, it has a lot of impacts, that is, let's take the example of insider trading. Some say that insider trading should not be banned. According to a radical liberalist, it should not be sanctioned because if I got information somehow it's okay for me to exploit it. Then if other market participants can't defend themselves, that's their problem. For example, a person doing office cleaning in an investment bank emptying the paper basket finds a virtually final contract of the merger between Fiat and Volkswagen. He steals nothing, he reads, and why couldn't he exploit this information, did he do something wrong? Actually, the theory says it is forbidden because the information he acquired it not through official channels but in connection with a function of it. But in a regulated world. In an absolutely liberal world, first come first served, that is, does the Texas potato farmer who found oil under his land have any special merit? My land is mine, under my land is oil, and I get the money. I found the information, I happened to find it like oil, why do you forbid me to use it? So in regulation, there are big ethical components. The exam questions generally are a theoretical part and a small case, which you don't have to judge, you have to dissect the topic quite thoroughly, even without arriving at a solution but representing the different advantages/disadvantages and the different categories of subjects that are affected by an ethical decision. So regulatory ethics have a big role in financial decisions as well. What I would like you to get to at the end of the course is to move from emotional intuition, which is good but you cannot rely on emotional intuition alone, to ethical reasoning. Uterus for rent, yes however there is something that doesn't add up, that is emotional intuition. Here you have to consider the problem on the basis of ethics. The last concept is that not only economic rules I can judge them on the basis of ethics but also vice versa, that is, ethical principles have economic consequences. For example, merit is important; it goes together with the concept of freedom. If I'm faster it's only fair that I get there before others if I'm taller I get the fruit that my shorter friend doesn't get to so I get to eat it, he doesn't. Do I have any merit in being taller or faster than another person? No. Merit is a complicated concept, so depending on how we treat conditions, there are economic consequences. The classic example, is why is it believed that an egalitarian world is better than a world of inequality? In a world of inequality, only children of lawyers can be lawyers. If you are the son of a servant you do the servant. This is believed to present less economic progress, so freedom improves one thing we like, economic progress. Because there might be a very good lawyer who is not a lawyer's son, and so if you don't intervene in the initial conditions you might have less development in society.

It is believed that freedom, by improving opportunities, improves progress. There is a person who could not study, who maybe would be a genius in programming, but we will never know. It is less frequent now because the whole world has become globalized but even in sports it can be like that, a person who does not play a certain sport because of social issues maybe could be a person who ran faster than everyone. We never knew that because maybe he had to spend his whole day doing something else. In this sense creating more just societies can give more development, so the economic setup influences ethical judgments but also vice versa.

Four children were born to Oedipus and Jocasta: two boys, Eteocles and Polynices, and two girls, Antigone and Ismene. Eteocles and Polynices, following their father's exile, were to share the regency of Thebes, thus establishing a diarchy in which they would both rule in alternating years. The first to hold the position of the ruler is Eteocles, who abuses his power by banishing Polynices from Thebes. Polynices thus organizes himself away from his native country and makes war on his brother. Creon, however, orders that only Eteocles be buried, pointing to Polynices as a traitor to his homeland. He also decides to punish with death anyone who disobeys his will and buries the body.

Antigone in a conversation with her sister Ismene objects to the unequal treatment of the two brothers' bodies and decides to take responsibility for burying Polynices. Ismene, who unlike Antigone is coolly rational and respectful of authority, tries to dissuade her sister and refuses to attend her brother's funeral.

The scene then shifts to Creon, to whom a guard reports that Polynices' body has been covered with sand. Creon is very irate and is convinced that the misdeed was done by some opponent, who must be tracked down and condemned.

The guard in order to discover the culprit digs up Polynices' body and hides to wait for someone to come forward to cover it: this is the ruler's niece, Antigone. When she is brought before Creon, Antigone accuses her uncle of placing himself by his decision above the gods; in fact, the funeral rite must be granted to all men by the will of the deities; not even a king can object to its being performed. Clearly, Antigone's accusations further exacerbate Creon's reaction, who condemns his niece to death. Ismene arrives and declares her willingness to share Antigone's fate, but Antigone reacts harshly as she has had to perform the funeral services without any support. The two sisters are then arrested. The populace shows solidarity with the young woman and Creon's son, Aemon, who is in love with and betrothed to Antigone, tries to intercede with his father. The conversation ends in disaster, Creon is cruel and adamant, and Aemon, deprived of any possibility of action, does not know how to help his beloved.

Creon then goes to Antigone to tell her that he has changed his decision: killing a member of her family is an act against nature that could arouse the wrath of the gods, so her fate will be to be imprisoned in a cave where she will remain as long as she lives. Creon, however, has already been guilty of a crime against the gods: refusing to give funeral services to Polynices.

He is reminded of his guilt by the soothsayer Tiresias, whom Creon hunts down, imputing to him that he wants to turn the situation in his favor. But Tiresias' words leave their mark on Creon's soul as he realizes the crimes against the family he is perpetrating. Eurydice, Creon's wife, then enters the scene, and a messenger who makes her aware of the tragic events that have shaken Thebes: Aemon had gone to free Antigone, but the young woman, not imagining that Creon might recant, had already hanged herself. Creon, who had just given a burial to Polynices, hears his son's cries and arriving in the cave just misses the attack of Aemon who, mad with grief, lashes out at his father. Aemon thus decides to kill himself and, facing Creon, stabs himself with his sword. Eurydice at the end of the account leaves the scene and Creon arrives, in the guise of her son. Shortly afterward he learns that Eurydice, having learned of Aemon's death, has killed herself in turn. The curtain thus falls on Creon, who, aware of his responsibility in his family's tragic end, pleads with the gods to give him death.

What moral laws are there in this tragedy? The first point is that there are divine rules, giving burial to dead people, and then there are as many rules, Creon's rules, which are civil rules, and social rules. So if one does a wrong thing and it was already known that the rule was that one cannot give burial to that person because it has to be left to the dogs and vultures, those who don't comply are punished. So two rules of behavior. Another thing you see in this tragedy, as also in Oedipus Rex, is that the dramaturgical aspect attracts attention because there is a dilemma, that is if the rules said when you are thirsty you drink, there would be no tragedy to write over such a rule. Problems arise when there are dilemmas, in this case, moral dilemmas.

And then one important thing is the question of authority, that is, authority dictates the rules, can one disobey these rules? For example, imagine the case of the whistleblower, that is, those who blow the whistle. An employee, doing his job, discovers things that he believes are wrong. This employee has two loyalty obligations so he is in a dilemma because the person who told him to do that thing, which is wrong for him, according to the company rules would have authority.

For example, you go to work and the head of operations, based on a piece of information that you know is confidential, tells you to build a position on a certain thing. You know that he had confidential information, what do you do? Do you call the Sec and report it, or do you play it cool and stick to your bank? These are cases where there is more than one authority, which authority do you obey if there is the conflict between authorities? It is a theme that for example is very clear in Antigone. The moral law of Antigone says that the dead should be buried. The law of the city says that those who have certain faults suffer certain consequences, and so we have dilemmas and obedience to authority, which can also occur in decisions in the world of finance and economics.

So much so that, for example, reporting one's superiors also enters into a discourse of convenience, that is, it is not just a discourse of what is right but what are the consequences that emerge. And in fact, within companies there are rules that they are obliged to comply with by external regulations, so for example there must be a confidential internal channel to report these issues. For example, if my boss tells me to sell strange securities, I am subject to this commercial pressure, I could send a letter to Consob and say that things are not working well in this bank because for a whole series of circumstances the pressure on me is exaggerated. I'm blowing the whistle, so I'm not helping the bank place securities, I'm blowing up a mess. So whom am I loyal to? To my moral rule or to the bank's internal rule? There is a disagreement between moral/general rule and internal rule.

So moral situations have to be deepened and deepened with moral levels, for which the literature is very useful.

We as an approach begin by studying the thought of some ancient philosophers. General premise: in the ancient world the divine had a much greater impact, that is, events very often were traced back to a higher entity. Harari in his book says to be careful that ideologies could almost be represented as something that is transmitted, so it is not that if we now are nationalists, believe in free markets, etc. we are sure that 200 years from now there will not be another way of thinking. That's simply the way it is now, so we don't have to judge those philosophers that we now see a little bit as an infant stage of progress that we have gone toward.

The oldest is Confucius, a very Eastern philosophy, according to him, people live within a supreme order, which is nature. The order is given by this external subject, let's call it a supreme being, and people are responsible for how they react. That's where ethics comes in. And of course, if there is a higher order we would think or rather we would prefer to think that it is good, that is, that the world is governed by good and not evil. One thinks that the world is governed by good and then something bad happens every now and then, not the other way around. So there is evil, but the higher order is good. So Confucius says we are governed by nature but reactions to the natural order are our own. Nature gives us our destiny, no one chooses where, or how we are born, many things that heavily shape our lives are not under our control. We agree on this, that is, we have no credit and no blame for a lot of things that happen to us, in fact, if we think about it many of the things we think are ours, conquered, are actually given. For example one could say Cristiano Ronaldo has talent, however, get the deck because he doesn't eat, he doesn't drink, and he trains. Maradona also knew how to play soccer however he was not so attentive. Then one says okay well it may have been the talent and everything else however he is also a very serious person. But beware that being like that might not be his merit, it is a characteristic. So many of the things that we think are our merit actually are not. The ability to focus or sacrifice, which means the ability to train or the ability to learn and follow a coach's instructions is a psychological characteristic. So is not having this ability. So nature, what is given, represents a lot. So there are things that come from outside, and the only thing we can govern, in part, is the reaction. According to Confucius, the main rule of behavior that one must follow is of "do not do to others what you would not want to be done to you." The first ethical rule we set up is this, the oldest one.

How should I behave? Meanwhile, I must not do the things that, in reverse, I would not want to be done to me. Another thing we draw is that Confucius was very concerned about the social aspect, that is, you have to maintain harmonious relationships with others, and the social basis for Confucius is the family. And the most important bond is the vertical bond, which means the generational obligations, so respecting elders, raising children, etc. again by the same token, you say elders are a burden, yes but someday you might be elderly yourself and so if you behave that way, in reverse is how you would like others to behave with you.

And so then horizontally, in other social structures, the same thing applies, so basically, the rule of Confucius is altruism. Then there are typically Eastern aspects like self-control or observance of rituals, which are needed to behave well. The other interesting thing about Confucius on rituals is that they are typically passed down from one generation to the next, so there is this vertical line of passing down rituals that are centered on the family and yet influence the whole society.

So according to Confucius, one should never do anything that alters the ritual, that is, the set of permissible rules. Ritual in our language of finance, economics could be precisely the set of rules and practices. It doesn't say in any law to respond to e-mails within a day, however in business you have to respond even faster, so behave according to rituals. The first rule of behavior: the importance of the social nucleus, family, and the rituals that convey the rules. In addition, we are responsible for how we react to the external order, which pre-exists!

The most influential strand of ethical thought in antiquity is that of Socrates and Plato. They are the same because Plato wrote the dialogues as Socrates, who had left nothing written.

We are around 400 B.C. in Athens, Socrates' principle is that you have to decide what to do based on whether it is right or not, not based on whether it is convenient or not. The moral rule is: a good man, in this condition, how would he behave?

That is, what would be the typical behavior of a good person? So one must do not what is convenient but what a good person would do. Socrates' second point is that if you know what is good, you do it. So you can only do wrong things if you do not have accurate knowledge of what is good-this is called "ethical intellectualism." So knowledge can be transmitted by teaching and therefore virtue can also be transmitted, because once you know what is good, you do it. And so the only cause of evil is ignorance of good because any subject who knows accurately what is good will want to do it because he will realize that it is the thing that attracts him most: this concept is defined by the Greek word "eudaimonia." I can understand that this kind of approach that I take seems to you to be a little bit distant in time, it is also a kind of approach that is a little bit distant from what we have in mind because there is someone to tell us what good is. But it is useful as a benchmark, you always have to keep in mind that there are alternative ways of looking at reality, for example, based on the concept of "good life." There is such a thing as not a fun life, a pleasant life, but it is a good life to strive for. One of my goals in these lectures is to make you grasp that to some extent what comes to mind we can always submit it to other points of view.

At the moment when one has to make a decision, look at that decision from the various points of view and not take them for granted, consider them as a product of the rules that are there at that moment, that is to say, we consider this decision according to the various people who are affected by this decision and according to the various points of view. One detail, how do we reach the knowledge of good and evil? According to Socrates, through debate. You will remember the dialogues of Socrates written by Plato that deal with various issues dialogically.

This is important because if you can come to find out what is good and what is evil by dialoguing with your fellow man, it means that the concept of good and evil is already within, that is, if good and evil are identified through dialogue, it means that we innately know what is good and what is evil. Clearly this is a way of looking at things that can be criticized. For example, evolutionary criticism says that simply these rules of good and evil are what allow us to coexist, so they have been selected by evolution. There is no god or we innately have awareness of what is good and what is evil. Killing is evil. One might say it is an action that is repugnant to us and therefore we have it in us.

But actually according to the most radical evolutionists this may be related to the fact that if there were someone who thought killing was good, you don't make a very large and cohesive society with people who enjoy killing because sooner or later they are left alone. The example is the sheep is a quiet animal. But is the sheep a quiet animal or did the sheep that ran away no longer reproduce and so the shepherds kept only the ones that didn't run away? It's more convenient to have 100 sheep than to have 10, but if they run away you have to spend your time running after the ones that run away, so the ones that run away you let them go and you keep the others that keep reproducing because they don't run away.

So according to some radical thinkers the way thinking has evolved does not depend on whether there is something good or bad per se, but simply because there are so many of us, who live in community, destructive thoughts such as stealing, telling lies, or killing, which are what we consider evil, from a radical point of view one might even say that these are not behaviors compatible with a social cohesion such as that which has developed in the community of human beings who talk about these things. Because if it were admitted that all people steal, and enter other people's houses to steal, surely there would be no cities, no dwellings. In the ancient world, this thing was not thought. It was thought this is the reality, look how well it works because it pre-exists, it comes from an otherworldly world or it is in the nature of people.

Another example that can be given besides sheep is, what is the nature of the Doberman? Is he a shy dog? No. But it is not in its nature; it was selected that way. The golden retriever is not aggressive but because when an aggressive one is born they don't breed it. The shy Doberman that does not attack is not made to breed.

So one cannot say what is the nature of the Dobermann, but how you selected Dobermann, it is a little bit different. So on the Doberman and the sheep we're comfortable, but who's to say that somehow we haven't self-selected in the same way? And so that what we think of as moral rules are a bit like aggression for the Doberman and gregarious spirit for the sheep?

We need to think about that. This is to distinguish philosophies that think there is good and evil and these are either preexisting or innate, from philosophies that are much more brutal and say you do what is convenient. So you don't have to make false budgets not because it's bad, but because if you make false budgets then people don't trust you anymore. For example, is the underworld a place where it is evil, but there are no rules? For example, the underworld is an extremely meritocratic environment. So the rules that are used are the rules that are used to run that kind of society: you do what you need to do, so much so that even in completely bad organizations like the criminal ones, according to a judgment of good or evil, there are rules and very often they are very sharply enforced.

Very well, so Socrates is of the first group, there is good and evil. Socrates in this is very radical, he even comes to paradoxes for example in the Critique which is one of his works he talks about this thing: if you can, can you avoid the death sentence by running away?

You know Socrates had been sentenced to death, his disciples said okay fine but run away and he says it is not right to run away because the rule is that you have to obey the laws, and so if it is unjust to run away because you are not obeying the rule, you don't have to do it even if it is convenient. So according to this rule, it is more moral to suffer an unjust conviction than to run away because Socrates didn't think he was wrong, he thought he was convicted in obeying the rules.

And because according to him the rules are more important than the person, it was not right to run away. So you have to do the right things and not look at the consequences. And in his intellectualism, once you know something is right, you don't want to do the wrong thing anymore, because if you know the good you can't wish to do the bad.

Socrates' was a very advanced philosophy. In another work one of his disciples tells him all this moral code of yours is actually propaganda, that is, many weak people designed the social order to prevent the strong from taking everything.

Whereas if you have a completely free system, that system will be enormously unequal, precisely because the initial conditions are not distributed according to criteria of justice. And even that can have an effect. So the objection to Socrates was: that the weak invent the rules to prevent the strong from taking too much advantage of them.

If you will this has also been seen in recent history, with aberrations such as with the Nazis: there are some people who are better than others and these people have to rule the world. So the weak is chain the strong with rules. In the opposite case: justice can be the system by which the powerful preserve the order they have achieved.

This way of representing reality can also be correct. From this other point of view, it is also true that the rules are made by those in charge, so they are also invented and used by the strong to subjugate the weak. Faced with these two extreme situations, Socrates gets away with the comparison of the city: if a thing was, there was a reason why it was that way. He would say do you see how the city works? In the city at the end there are 3 classes of citizens. The ruling class, who are right to rule because they know they want the good of the city.

The auxiliary class, of the military, is needed to make sure that good ideas and the good of the city can be realized. In the sense that the police, the military, is needed. Then there is the class of peasants, artisans, merchants who take care of material goods. Since this thing is like this, it is right that it should be like this. Keep in mind that in those days there was slavery, and any thinker of the time however brilliant and highly intelligent thought that since slaves are there, it was right that there should be slavery.

If you look at it from that point of view, if you think that if something is there, it's because it responds to some higher order, when I was born there were slaves and therefore it means there must be. It's not that they thought that after 2,000 years there wouldn't be any more, according to them slaves had always been there and therefore it was normal for them to be there.

Since the city has these 3 classes, the justice is for everyone to do their job, everyone must perform the function for which they are suited, but what is the function for which you are suited? It is that of the class in which you are placed. What is the definition of a tailor? One who can sew well. The order is for everyone to do well the task in which they are placed. Good is doing well the job in which you are in. Clearly if you put a housekeeper to be a tailor he is not capable or if you put a tailor to be a housekeeper he is not capable.

This is a demonstration of the fact that, in an orderly society, everyone has to do the role that is intended for him. We come to the soul, the soul also has 3 parts according to Socrates.

Reason is the government, that is, it decides what is right and what is wrong. At the lowest level are instincts, some instincts may not be for the good of the individual. For example, the instinct to drink to drunkenness may not be the best for the health of the body. To reduce the conflicts that arise in the soul there is what he called the heart, which tries to govern these two things.

Because when faced with certain things that maybe we are attracted to, for example one makes me angry and I kill him. But this thing disturbs me a little bit, so the heart tells me it's not right. And then the intermediary between what I know is right and instinct/passion is given by this consciousness, by feeling. So the conflicts are there, how do we resolve them? Socrates and all the ancient thinkers that we will see have this problem of the preestablished order. If you have a preconstituted order then you have a hard time fitting everything into it, and so to say that it's enough to know good to do it is in conflict with the fact that there are people who do evil, even knowing it's evil.

So you have to make up this thing about the city and the 3 components. But he says precisely that true happiness is when the soul is ordered, that is, when reason rules, instead the example of a debating subject is a subject prey to the passions.

So moral virtue is doing what you know to be good, and the passions are resolved with this theme of the breakdown of the soul in which there is the reason, instincts, and the heart.

According to Aristotle, an action is virtuous if it leads to stability of the soul and thus to a stable character. What is good character?

We are what we repeatedly do. Excellence then is not an act but a habit. It means that it is not that excellence or goodness is an inherent thing, it is something we achieve, we get used to it. To achieve good character one has to work by removing obstacles.

So Aristotle's goal remains the good life, but the good life is achieved precisely by getting used to doing good things.

A good subject is not that he is good or he is not good, a good subject is one who does good things. It is a pragmatic type of logic. Like Socrates and Plato, virtue equals the good life. The virtuous person understands the right things and judges them to be right and is attracted to the right things, so the good is also attractive, but in order to achieve it one must exercise good deeds.

So it's a more pragmatic approach than Plato's, it's not a matter of understanding what the good is and then automatically you will practice the good once you understand it, according to Aristotle I get used to doing good things and then I become good. And so habit develops character. According to Aristotle there are also bad habits, but what he means is an active habit, not a passive habit.

One can also get used to things that he knows are bad, for example getting used to a scruffy life. So he kind of reverses the approach of Socrates and Plato who say: a good person is one who does good things. Aristotle says: to know if a person is good I look at what he does, if he does good things habitually it means he is good.

Another Aristotelian concept is that the right thing has teleological characteristics, which means it looks at the end of things. A thing is good, therefore it is right if it achieves the end for which it exists. For example, a good characteristic of the flute is to produce good sounds. It is right for those who are able to extract good sounds from the flute to play the flute.

So Aristotle's concept of merit is this. It is right that he should administer the city who administers it well, and he who administers it well who repeatedly has proven to administer it well. So justice is teleological, who is just to do certain things and have certain goods or even certain benefits? He who makes the best use of it for society. According to Aristotle, the highest activity that a person can do is political activity, and therefore it is right for those who are best at it to govern. As a second thing justice in addition to being teleological is also honorific, that is, it is proper for something to be done if it has an honorific character, that is, if it is assigned to whom I wish to report it is proper to be assigned. This thing of honorific justice is quite interesting, I am reminded of a case that is in the news these days.

It is the case of the rich American gentlemen who were bribing universities to get their children in, there is one

ongoing scandal. In America, the university system is very selective and also very expensive, but you realize the issue that if one comes out of that university then one makes a lot of careers and earns a lot of money, if one comes out of another university much less and so anyway everybody wants to go to the major universities.

We were always told that there are selections, so everything meritocratic. After that it turns out that if one made a significant enough donation to the university, one still got in. So what is the ethical problem? The line of course is very thin because if you are an average intelligent person and you also have a lot of money, you can even take courses to prepare for the entrance exam or you can pay for a professor to teach you something, already money matters even then.

On the other hand, if you're someone who lives in a trailer and has to work four hours a day, it's a lot harder than someone who lives in New York and is a child of the big person who can spend money.

After that there is this scandal that some people were paying admission. Obviously if you pay admission there is a problem, you have to figure out if you have ruined the common good of believing on the merits. Maybe it's a myth, but we've been told that if you're good enough and you try hard enough then you can get results. So already this news ruins the myth and so you have a damage anyway. Second thing, if merit counts for anything, because there is closed number, if 5 children of rich people get in it means that 5 who were good anyway but are not children of rich people stay out.

So because those professions are also sometimes important professions, like law, economics or medicine, you're going to have 5 doctors who are not as good as the other 5 who didn't have the important parents and so society loses out. But going back to Aristotle, he wouldn't be happy with that because you wouldn't have met the end. Selection exists to promote the best, because we think that those who rank high in the test rankings are then the people who will become the best doctor or the best lawyer.

Justice must also be honorific, so what does the university then do? That's a good question, because if the person who is the best at taking the exams wins at the university, then you have to have a test that provides for that thing well. But if the university is for something else, what is the virtue you want to prevail? What is the virtue you want to reward? According to Aristotle the flute you have to give it to the best musician to play, not the one who has the most money to buy it because the nature of the flute is to produce beautiful sounds.

So justice is teleological (what is it for) and honorific (what signal do I send to others, if I want people to study music I must give to play the flute not to the one who has the most money to buy it but to the one who plays it best). Since the ultimate goal is to live well, to live well is to live in accordance with the principle of justice. According to Aristotle, the characteristic function of man compared to other animals is the reason.

Since man is characterized by reason one must choose what is in accord with reason. The good for man is that which accords with reason. Happiness is acting in accordance with reason. The reason, however, must be nurtured through habit. This is why the highest human activities are those that have to do with reason, not enjoyment. The best subjects are politicians and scholars because they make the most use of reason.

Since, according to Aristotle, nature does nothing in vain, that is, if something is there, it is because there is an underlying law, happiness is the use of reason without excess. The theory of the right middle, every human characteristic lies between two extreme elements, for example courage is a middle virtue because it lies between cowardice and recklessness. Because a courageous person knows the dangers, but he can overcome them with reason and take calculated risks, otherwise he would be reckless, or if he never wants to expose himself he would be cowardly. A thrifty person is somewhere between a spendthrift and a miser.

According to Aristotle, virtue is being in the middle. And since Aristotle has pragmatic ideas, as we said before, according to him ethical virtue works well only when it is associated with actions, thus with practical thinking.

Other minor currents of thought are the **cynics**. The idea is simple life, Diogenes anecdote. Alexander the Great visits the philosopher Diogenes and says I am the most powerful man in the world, what can I do for you? And Diogenes answers if you please move out of the sun you are shadowing me. So he was not interested in riches, material possessions, etc., and so for the cynics the goal of life is detachment from earthly things, not being conditioned by earthly things, detachment from transient possessions. This later will become very important for Stoicism.

Not to be dominated by the passions, to be able to detach oneself from material goods: this was the virtue for the cynics, so essentiality.

The opposite are the **Cyrenaics** who say the goal of life is pleasure. What pleasure, long-term pleasure? No the immediate pleasure. There is no gradation of pleasure. You can't say that going to a classical music concert is better than wolfing down fries and ketchup, if I like wolfing down fries and ketchup better, there is no superior and inferior pleasure, it just depends on what one wants to do.

So pleasures do not differ, they have gradations only in terms of desirability, not in terms of higher goods and lower goods. One thinks that going to the Scala is better than going to the stadium, but according to the Cyrenaics it is not so. You do what gives you the most pleasure.

The evolution of the Cyrenaics are the **Epicureans**. Epicurean moral theory is the best known hedonistic moral theory in ancient philosophy. Hedonistic means based on pleasure. These sound like high school concepts, but in economics and finance this thing is used a lot, because it is the principle of utility at the end. What is to be done? What leads to the greatest degree of satisfaction. Compared to the Cyrenaics who thought about pleasure per se, according to the Epicureans true pleasure is that which leads to virtue. Because according to Epicurus all desires are not equal, some were good and some were natural.

Among the natural ones were those that were simply natural and those that were necessary. Necessary natural desires are those that solve an uncomfortable situation, for example one is thirsty and drinks. Unnecessary natural desires are for example I drink carbonated water or wine. For Epicurus unfounded desires were desires for honors, statues, esteem of other people.

The purpose of life according to Epicureans was freedom from pain, so not to achieve pleasures in positive terms but to eliminate pain. What we are interested in, beyond these introductory things is how is society then organized? How is society decided on the basis of this pleasure principle? One has to organize in such a way that the harm done to the other is minimized. So the fundamental rule is pleasure, but pleasure as freedom from pain, need, etc. not the pleasure of the Cyrenaics as any kind of pleasure. And so in this sense society must be organized in such a way as to avoid harming others.

One set of thinkers who had an even greater impact on later philosophy are the **Stoics**. According to the Stoics there is a principle that governs the universe, which is what they called logos.

This principle that governs the universe is virtue. To be happy one must lead a virtuous life. Material goods are not needed; in this they are related to the cynics. Material goods are not necessary for happiness and therefore in themselves material goods are neither good nor bad. The reasoning they make is that since any material good can be used for good or for evil, they can be neither good nor bad in themselves.

And good, on the other hand, must invariably be good. Also according to the Stoics, virtue is a habit, so the wise subject acts according to reason. He can experience joy when he acts according to reason, but not pleasure because pleasure is not a virtue according to the Stoics.

As for **skeptics**, let us take up only one concept that is very useful for analysis. Skepticism means suspension of judgment and

continuous search, that is, I can never be sure whether something is good or bad by nature. One must suspend judgment and have detachment from passions.

Suspension of judgment is an important issue because one of the main mistakes one can make in judging ethical situations involving finance is to judge too quickly. Suspension of judgment leads, according to skeptics, to peace of soul, what is called "ataraxia" so absence of perturbations and passions.

A major phenomenon then erupted, which is Christianity, which has had a gigantic impact on Western ethical thought, particularly connected with Platonic and Stoic ideas. The first important Christian ethical philosopher is St. Augustine of Hippo.

Christian philosophers had one problem more than others, which was the justification of evil, that is, God created the world, God is good. Did God also create evil? If he was a good God, how does he also create evil? So they had this relevant problem.

Augustine solves it by saying that there is the city of men (earthly peace is pursued) and the city of god (eternal peace is pursued).

Good men dwell in the city of god, evil men dwell in the city of men. So what is the theme of evil? The theme of evil is not in the things of the world, because God created them. So greed is not the fault of gold but it is the fault of people's immoderation, it is the fault of people's bad judgment.

Another somewhat complicated distinction he made is between the intelligible world, that is, the world of thought, and the sensible world, that is, the material world. The intelligible world works well if we understand it, whereas the sensible world is subject to the effects of impermanence, it can become corrupted, we can make mistakes in the material world.

So the sensible world is not evil in itself, our problem is a problem of will so evil exists, error exists because of a defect of will that goes back to people's sin. So we are wrong when we judge evil, the will is good but the judgment can be wrong.

Moral evil is man's will when he turns away from God and attaches himself to lower goods instead of higher goods, so evil is a subtraction from a higher will. This element of the will is Augustine's main focus. A big part of his philosophy is about free will, in modern terms we will call it "decision theory" for this we are interested in. In his world this is complicated because how do you reconcile the fact that there is a God who knows everything with the free will of man who makes mistakes?

If man errs it can only be his fault, because since God knows everything, the moral responsibility can only be man's. The theme is that there is a reality, people can misjudge it, and they can make mistakes.

This issue is taken even further in Thomas Aquinas, who is a bit of a middle ground between Aristotle and Christian doctrine.

In that following Aristotle he says that an act is good/bad depending on whether it brings us closer to/farther from the true human god, but at the same time true happiness, true purpose is achieved not in this life but in supernatural union with God.

And so in this dialectic between the human condition, original sin, etc. and the tendency toward God lies the idea of Thomas, who says: the things that exist are good because God created them, people can make bad decisions especially if they rely on earthly things since earthly things are corruptible.

The most interesting part of St. Thomas' philosophy is the "double effect theory." Why is a decision criterion important? The double effect is: you want to do a good thing and that has side effects. We are interested because we are always interested in dilemmas, we have to decide between two things. Can a given action have negative effects? For example I open a steel mill, I create jobs, but I pollute.

And so a good thing and a bad thing. There is a company in crisis, I have to reduce costs, to reduce costs I have to lay off people, in this way I save the company but eliminate the hundred salaries for families who need them. What criteria does Thomas identify for analyzing situations like this?

The double effect theory says as a first thing that the bad result must not be sought, I must not want to pollute or not care that I pollute or I must not want to lay off people and find the excuse that the company is in crisis. As a second thing it must be proportionate that is, the bad effect must not be greater than the positive effect sought. Then the negative action must not be unacceptable, for example it is not that to save a company I can kill 100 people, there are some things that cannot be done.

The intention must be good, it must be to achieve good, not a neutral or negative intention disguised under positive aspects. So to recapitulate, the side effect of the action must not be prohibited, so there are some things I cannot do.

Second, the purpose of the whole action must be positive, so the negative side effect must really be a side effect, it must not be among the goals of the action. The intention must be good so everything must be done to minimize the negative effect, but if the intention was negative or instrumental even the positive effect would not be enough to justify the negative aspect.

And then there is proportionality, the cost of the negative action must not be disproportionate to the positive effect. This theory of double effect was developed in Thomas Aquinas and we say it characterizes the generality of economic decisions, because there is always some negative effect. Sometimes it may be the case that we try to mask some negative action with a patina of positive varnish, and by using Aquinas' double-effect decision criterion, this helps us in many cases to get an idea about the acceptability or otherwise of various actions. Let's turn to more recent times.

A website would damage Mrs. Trump because she would do interviews saying that when she was modeling she also went to dinner, etc. The problem is that in the quote he says meanwhile with that story, you website made money.

Plus the damage he is complaining about is not only on his honor, but it is on the fact that the lady's brand has lost a lot of value and that value is very high because the lady had the only opportunity to be a very famous, very well-known person and therefore to be able to advertise accessories, shoes, jewelry, cosmetics, etc.

What is it here that we are not convinced about from an ethical point of view? If you were the judge, what might you think? In the harm that you have done to me what do we put?

So it's not that she says but I when I go home my son who knows how he looks at me, however she also says that she missed opportunities that will never happen again to enhance her brand Melania Trump, because this was at the beginning of the presidency. There is an extra passage here than normal. We imagine that you are right, however on the determination of harm there is something more. How would one respond using one of the thinkers we have already seen?

In Aristotle's approach for example, being the wife of the president of the United States, the nature of being first lady is there that she must be respected because she represents a nation, etc. It is in her nature. But it's not in the nature of being first lady to exploit that position to sponsor her own brand, that part is one more thing from an ethical point of view.

Americans are very sensitive to this aspect of the benefits attached to the office. So much so that they are very much criticized for example the former presidents of the United States who after their term in office do conferences, consultancies, etc. because they say you don't do them because you are good, but because having been president of the United States you are exploiting the notoriety to put money in your pocket. That money would be from the position, not yours. If you've been a major figure at the Fed you can't immediately afterwards go and work in a bank because it's clear that if that's the case, those who want to influence your decisions afterwards will promise to hire you. There is also a message issue, i.e. if I want to bribe the authorities, I don't have to buy all the exponents, just buy some that sends the message that if you don't treat me very badly then maybe you might get some advantage.

Coming back to us, Aristotle says things should be used for the reason for which they are stated. The first lady is not paid to advertise or sell goods, but she is paid because having to be the wife of the president of the United States she cannot do other jobs. So it is only fair that if someone offends you, that someone has to be punished and then you have to be compensated, we have to see if we can go as far as perfumes, etc.

So as you see, even in very recent and curious cases there are implications that our ethical judgment can attach to. This has to do with Aristotle.

There is a fairy tale about a vain emperor who is completely devoted to taking care of his outward appearance, particularly his clothing.

One day two swindlers who had come to the city spread the rumor that they were weavers and had at their disposal a new and formidable fabric, thin, light and wonderful, with the peculiarity of being invisible to fools and the unworthy.

The courtiers sent by the king cannot see it; but lest they be misjudged, they report to the emperor praising the magnificence of the fabric. The emperor, convinced, has the tricksters prepare a suit of clothes for him. When this is delivered to him, however, the emperor realizes that he is not able to see anything either; attributing the non-seeing of the fabric to his own unworthiness that he himself knows, and like his courtiers before him, he too decides to pretend and show himself enraptured by the work of the weavers.

In his new dress he parades through the streets of the city in front of a crowd of citizens who applaud and praise the elegance of the ruler, although they see nothing either and feel that they themselves are secretly guilty of unconfessed unworthiness. The spell is broken by a child who, widening his eyes, cries out innocently, "but the king has nothing on!" from which comes the famous phrase "The king is naked!" Nevertheless, the ruler continues undaunted to parade as if nothing had happened.

We need this to introduce a topic, in the ancient thinkers we have seen so far the way of thinking was somewhat self-referential.

There is some preexisting idea, so good and evil exist, we understand them through reasoning. In the continuation of thinking about ethical issues, however, another theme is introduced, which is that there is a thought to think, so if we are good enough we think it, but the thought is already there.

That is, God is there, the world is right. In St. Augustine there is this issue, and that is all that matters is written in the Bible. Then someone pops up and says but in the Bible there is never any mention of spiders, yet spiders are there. St. Augustine's answer is I don't care, it's because the spider is not relevant, i.e. if God didn't put it in the Bible it means it doesn't matter, we don't have to debate this thing.

The extra step is that actually we can say that man is capable of being wrong by himself, indeed in being wrong I can be very much influenced by others as happens in the emperor's new clothes.

Because first these dishonest merchants come and say a false thing. However in saying a false thing they are also shrewd and say this cloth is so beautiful that only those who really understand so much can see it. And so the guards at the city gates, in order not to look like fools and especially knowing that the king is very vain, they don't take the risk of saying you are cheaters, go away. So these present themselves well, tell a convincing story. The guardians on the one hand are afraid of passing as unintelligent and are also afraid of the king's judgment. This story is interesting because in the ethics of finance it happens a lot. Imagine there is a 'CEO who says this year I want to make $10 billion in profits and he says it at the beginning of the year. And everybody knows it.

The CEO presents to the board of directors this fantastic business plan and the board members say but are we sure we're going to make all these profits? Let's pretend that we believe that we will be able to sell all our electric cars. This question is important first of all from a sociological point of view, and really it works like this, our moral judgment is influenced by what we think other people think-this thing is called conformism.

So the ancient philosophers just thought that there was right and wrong, it's not that if we all agree on something wrong then it becomes right. In Aristotle there is no such concept. In Plato there is even the opposite, that is, the judgment that the court in Athens gives to Socrates is wrong, but Socrates says it is right to obey the judgment even if it is wrong. Instead more modern psychology shows this aspect, so there is the theme of conformity.

Then the other theme is that no one takes the initiative to break the path even if something seems really wrong to them. So evil can spread even for trivial reasons. A business can be mismanaged and one can say but is it possible that no one notices? It is not necessary, that is, it could happen that someone notices or even everyone notices, but only those who come from outside and are not conditioned by what others think have the courage to report it.

The other thing this fairy tale shows us is that the one who has the courage to report it is the child, but because he has nothing to lose. For example, a teacher divides the class into two groups and to some he says you are the guardians, to the others you are the prisoners. After a while the environment degenerates because the guards were misbehaving with the others.

An experiment makes people in certain environmental conditions do things that people not in that environment would find completely absurd. The previous theory was: it's not the environment, it's people self-selecting. This experiment challenged that, showed how the environment makes everyone adhere to their role. Another example of conformity. This is interesting to us because one says Titius was wrong and we don't consider the environment he was in. This experiment makes us say watch out let's see what the retail influences are.

Then there is the concept of escalation, that is, from a small concession follow larger and larger concessions. We had left behind an interesting thing regarding Islam, we are interested in the concept of "riba" (prohibition of interest) and "gharar." It is a religious thought and so it is based on a concept of equality between people. So the concept of symmetry. Meanwhile, property, whose property is it? The property is God's, the world is God's, and people have custody of it.

And so you have to conserve it and distribute it according to principles of cooperation and social responsibility, which does not mean egalitarianism, but it means equality of opportunity, so everyone has to be remunerated according to his or her abilities and commitment.

Attached to this is a concept of blaming idleness, that is, you must get the right income for the work you do, but if the work is not found, it is your fault. The riba is the absolute prohibition of interest, money cannot grow, if someone makes it grow he commits a wrong thing. More interesting is the concept of gharar, the prohibition against making money on uncertainty.

While riba is absolute prohibition, excessive gharar is not allowed.

So for example, is it permissible to sell the fruits of a field before they are harvested? Yes because the uncertainty is not excessive, I see the trees, I see there are fruits, which are not ripe, in a month they will ripen. So there is uncertainty because if it hails the fruits are no longer good, however, the two parties suffer from the same uncertainty. Whereas asymmetric contracts are prohibited because they suffer from excessive gharar. If there are excessive information asymmetries these contracts fall under the prohibition of gharar.

Derivative contracts have a difficult life in Islam because lottery is forbidden in Islamic thought, so all types of bets are forbidden by the religion. When a derivative comes too close to a bet, then it is forbidden. The ancient thinkers for a very long time thought that what there was to know was already known, you just had to think it better, it was written in the Bible or the Quran. You just had to be good at thinking it better and explaining it better.

Even the Greek philosophers thought things were innate. With the scientific revolution, which happened to develop along with geographical discoveries, people completely changed their way of thinking, and that is, they began to think that they did not know everything. We don't think we know everything, but we think there will still be things to be discovered. In the ancient world it was not like that, that is, what you needed to know you already knew. Then you had to study to learn, pass on, understand, interpret, etc. The medieval scholar is someone who reads books, not experiments. It was with the Renaissance that they began to question what was known. Having reached this point, one questions what one knows.

Now we start with a character named Spinoza. We start with Aristotle: a thing is good, if it is good it is perfect, unaffected, so a perfect thing gives us power to act. What is evil? A thing that impedes our power to act. So a thing is good if it gives us power to act, it is evil if it hinders our power to act.

Obviously in the Christian tradition the highest good is to be able to know God, so the highest power, the highest perfection is knowledge. Man tends to know God, so the highest good is knowledge. Distinction between soul and body, the soul acts according to final causes, the body acts according to efficient causes. Everything would be orderly if there was no free will, that is, if it were that everything works this way, final causes, efficient causes, knowledge of God, etc. we would all get along. The problem is that any philosopher who starts from these premises conflicts with the fact that people then mess up, i.e., evil exists and wrong things exist, which come from free will. According to Spinoza, free will is the basis of ethics.

This is what we are interested in, that is, there is no ethics without free will. Because if the world were all ordered the way God thought of it, since God is not that he can make mistakes, everything would be all right, because all physical structures are in agreement with each other.

Keep in mind that until Darwin the prevailing thought was that things worked a certain way because God made them that way, one would say look at the intelligence that God had that made the giraffe because that's how it eats the leaves off the trees, if

[162]

it had a short neck it would have starved to death. That's true, I mean if you see it that way it's right.

Darwin says another thing, that by dint of going through generations, in that place where there were the trees with the good leaves up, the giraffes with short necks died, the ones with long necks reproduced and so now you see that in that environment there is an animal that has a long neck. And so you say look how well it works, it doesn't, the causation is different. All this until Darwin was not there, you say look how well the world works, every effect has its cause. There are prey and predators, look how well the universe was created. In the cold there are animals with fur, in the water there are fish, etc. Then the world is so perfect that there is no room for error, and so evil comes from free will. But do we really have a choice, says Spinoza?

Sometimes it seems to us that a certain decision is absolutely made by us. The problem is that he says this is always true, even when one is drunk or it seems to us that he has some form of dementia or a child. So even those who we think are judging wrongly are judging right in their heads.

So according to Spinoza there are both external and internal causes that determine our actions. So this question of free will basically comes down to the fact that we struggle to accept the fact that we are conditioned. Because one may think that I cannot decide whether I have a lot of hair or a little hair, whether I am tall or short, but how I behave I can decide. Then one has to take into consideration that if there is free will, our actions, which involve punishments, rewards, justices, are affirmed within the framework of society, thus the state. According to Spinoza if everyone acted according to reason, if everyone was rational etc. there would be no need for the state. Since this is not the case, the presence of a state is needed. And only in the context of a society can the concept of good or evil according to Spinoza be conceived.

What he calls "ethical egoism" that is, everyone tends to self-assert himself, ethical egoism finds tempering in society, in the fact that there is a state. So everyone is free to seek his own advantage, one can be obliged to do only what one is able to do. Being embedded in a context of society, we have to balance this ethical selfishness with the collective good.

We will take up the passage later with utilitarian philosophers. There are two kinds of utilitarianism, there is animal utilitarianism and utilitarianism that looks more in the long run. Animal utilitarianism is that one gets drunk, eats like a pig, however, one does not get to that because one thinks that the next morning one is sick for example.

Or one tells lies, arrives late to appointments, however, then if others realize that is the case, then it doesn't suit him. So there is immediate utilitarianism and utilitarianism that looks in the long run. Immediate utilitarianism according to Spinoza would be ethical egoism, I have to just look at myself. But since living alone in the end is more exhausting than living within a society, it is better for me to have a state that limits me because in any case the overall utility is greater than in the opposite case.

This is a fairly important principle of finance, when we say for example that honesty is the best business policy, "honesty is the best policy." There is always a fairly fine line between telling the truth and not telling the truth, or telling the whole truth or telling part of the truth. The principle is you don't copy on exams.

Aristotle tells you no copying on exams. Spinoza's ethical egoism says I decide whether or not you copy on exams. Animal utilitarianism says of course you copy so I don't study and go out the night before. The let's say commercial utilitarianism, from an advanced society, is I have to think it through because if I get the reputation that I copy, then maybe in ten years I happen to be out in the world in the workplace and on the other side of the table I find a former classmate of mine and he maybe says to his colleagues, let's trust this guy though he was a copycat all the time. Is it worth the risk to me today, to not study the last 3 days, to lose an important business in 10 years because I had the reputation of the one who didn't study and copied? So it is still utility, but it is a mediated utility. Coming back to us, society limits me, however, it is more convenient for me to be in society and therefore I have the rational impulse to act morally out of pure self-interest.

So to be ethical out of self-interest, not to adhere to norms or because it is right, but because it is convenient. The evolution of this concept is "moral contractualism," so we are moral because, by even implicit rules, we have determined to be that way. We have established to be on time, not to copy, to return the money we have been lent, etc. Not to do certain things because there seems to be an ethical motive, but in fact the real motive is convenience.

If we want to exaggerate, one of the worlds where they are most fixated on ethics is the world of investment banking, which is one of the most ruthless worlds from a people-to-people perspective. But they are fixated on ethics for the sake of reputation, because the cost of losing a deal is so high that it pays to behave well. It is therefore the social contract that makes us abide by ethical conventions. An example from Spinoza is why is suicide to be condemned?

Obviously according to religious doctrine it goes against the commandment not to kill so one should not even kill oneself. He says you don't need to go that far, but it is simply against ethical selfishness, it means you are weak, you didn't do your math right.

To be virtuous means to preserve your existence, so suicide is not a contravention of the commandment not to kill, but it is wrong from the point of view of ethical egoism. As well as ethical selfishness means that those who are rational always act honestly and do not deceive others. If deceiving was rational then you should always deceive, but if you always deceive it doesn't work, if everyone always told lies the world wouldn't work.

Another important English philosopher concerned with economics is Thomas Hobbes, according to him man is a mechanical animal whose only goal is self-interest, thus pure selfishness.

The only motive of human behavior is the pursuit of pleasure and trying to avoid pain. According to him these are the instincts, while the power of reasoning, that is, the power to react, to control these instincts leaves him quite skeptical. As for moral judgments he believes they are distorted by self-interest and the pleasures/pains of the moment.

And in particular he says something that I for one do not agree with, we are prone to use feelings and impulses as measures of judging the behavior of others. So we judge others' behavior and in our heads we make a rational representation of it. We are moved in our judgment by our feelings and inclinations. In addition, Hobbes is very skeptical that when we turn our reasoning away from real things, we are in danger of making reasoning that precisely loses touch with reality and thus set ourselves up to argue about abstract matters, even contradicting ourselves.

So we form beliefs about supernatural entities just out of fear, sentimental, impulse reasons, and taking this example shows how our judgment can be distorted. And another way in which our judgment can be distorted is on the basis of rhetorical arguments from our interlocutors. For example, the whole fascination with Socrates, if you read the Socratic dialogues there is a lot of rhetoric in the arguments, so the arguments that are made are based very much on inductive and dialectical reasoning but that tends to be detached from reality. So man is rationally selfish but at the same time he does altruistic things, and at the same time he also does things that are unnecessarily cruel and sometimes against his own interest.

And this in a utilitarian world is not justified. Against self-interest for example there are situations of personal revenge or wars, things that have no expediency and are self-destructive in nature. So Hobbes is very skeptical about man's judgment because we are led astray by our own attempts to understand something, we make mistakes in reasoning, our reasoning is based on language, so words influence us, before the battles the generals' speeches were driven by reasoning that distorts our will.

He also says that in this world, being so characterized, an important role is played by the state. Authority is a matter of convenience, since you live in a context of utilitarianism in which there are other people willing a little bit of everything, very shrewd and even the strongest/intelligent have to sleep, it is necessary to create some effective authority. So it is not necessary for everyone to be bad and violent, it is enough that there is someone who behaves badly and therefore rules and laws are needed more than morality to make sure that the state of nature is avoided and that the social whole can stay together.

Why should we obey the laws that a ruler makes? In contractualism one could say because I chose it, I made a voluntary contract and that in democracy applies. Worse is if there is not even democracy, that is, if these rules are not contractually chosen but are suffered. So being in a context where there are rules is important to make society work because otherwise many of the achievements of society do not work.

According to Hobbes, in a state of nature or with a weak state, only the weak obey the rules and only when they are obliged to do so. Only in an organization that has rules for example is the right to property respected, otherwise everyone would have to spend time guarding his property hoping to have the strength to defend himself. So society is only viable in the context of a state that forces me to abide by rules, beyond ethics.

In a world of gatherers/hunters it's not like you need a lot of rules, from farming onwards you need rules because otherwise no one is going to farm a field if someone comes along and takes away the fruit of a year's work. A picker on the other hand doesn't have this problem, the fruit he finds doesn't belong to anyone, he just takes it and eats it. So state of nature, rules that it is convenient for us to abide by, and pessimism about morality per se, instead morality as a convenient limit to the state of nature.

Also in England there is another character, which is John Locke. He says how is it that we form our ideas, so how is it that we judge whether something is to be done or not? We form our ideas in two ways, by sensation or by reflection. This is an important step forward from what we have been saying, because instead according to the ancient philosophers, ideas pre-exist, we have to investigate but they are innate.

According to him no, there are no innate ideas in the human mind, everything comes from sensation which is the great source of all ideas, and from reflection on the sensations we had. Locke is utilitarian so the way to judge ideas according to him comes from the satisfaction or discomfort we feel in thinking about them. So you start from the sensations, I put my hand on the fire: unpleasant, I don't have to do that anymore. I think I put my hand on the fire: unpleasant. And so putting someone's hand on fire is wrong. I start from the sensation, I reproduce the sensation, then I judge the goodness or badness of an act depending on this kind of satisfaction or discomfort I get from a thought.

So pleasure and pain characterize all our ideas, whether of sensation or thought. What makes us prefer one action to another, thus making us point to right and wrong are precisely sensations.

What is wrong is associated with the idea of pain, what is good with the idea of pleasure. Good is what increases pleasure or reduces pain, bad is what reduces pleasure or increases pain. Things we can experience or prefigure, that is, we can come to think about them. Locke then makes a self-criticism, he says imagine there is a subject who likes to tell lies, so for him telling the lie is associated with a positive idea, of pleasure. But clearly telling lies is not a good thing.

So there is a contradiction between I understand what is good depending on what I like, but if there is someone who likes something wrong is free to do these things, would society still function? Clearly not. So he gets away with distinguishing between "happiness" and "true happiness." He introduces in this way a hierarchy of pleasures; there are more worthy pleasures and less worthy pleasures. True happiness is the pursuit of the most worthy pleasures.

The example he gives is imagine that there is an unpleasant drug, clearly the feeling tells us not to take that drug but the real pleasure, that is, regaining health tells us take that drug. This allows us to make a general argument, there are two kinds of utilitarianism, there is the animal utilitarianism in which any pleasure is equal to another: going to hear a Beethoven concert is the same as watching an episode of The Simpsons.

Many people, however, think that there are different degrees of good things, and he belongs to this second category, that is, for Locke there is a gradation even in pleasures. To come to this conclusion he brings up the concept of judgment day. If there were no judgment day, if life stopped here, all pleasures would be on the same level. Since there is a judgment day there is no need to make choices that alter the eternal law, and so there is an orderly way to decide what is good and what is evil. And so there is a natural law that makes the whole world work and the rules set by the lawmakers, that is, the so-called positive law, conforms to this natural law. And so natural law causes there to be pleasures that are more in line with justice, with natural law rather than just pleasure.

Then he gives an example, he says the scholar who derives his pleasure from reading, from learning, from studying literature, then however he must also eat, drink, and when he does these things he prefers good food to less good food. Similarly, the glutton who is only interested in eating and good things will eventually have a desire for knowledge stimulated by the fact that he considers precisely the famous judgment day. On the wise it is quite convincing, on the gaiety he needs to resort to the concept of the day of judgment. Then how come we err, that is, how come we make wrong judgments?

Because it is difficult for us to compare immediate pleasures and pains with future pleasures and pains/reminders. He gives the example of things near and things far, we can judge things near well, when they are far we judge them poorly, for example if every glass of alcohol was accompanied by a headache that follows after a few hours everything would be easier. We have to rely on moral rules to improve judgments that our minds, not being trained to consider remote consequences, have a hard time judging. And so we need to convince people that virtue and religion are things to follow because it's convenient, even though I don't immediately see the convenience.

So according to him morality is about overcoming this mistake that our mind would have us make, that is, if we don't have immediate feedback we have a hard time deciding correctly a cognitive problem. No one puts a cigarette out on his hand because it hurts immediately, however, he smokes even if he knows it hurts in the future, because he does not have the immediate feedback.

So there must be rules to limit behavior even if that behavior is welcome. This kind of utilitarianism is embedded in a longer-term context and thus overcomes the selfishness typical of pure utilitarianism.

Important German philosopher is Gottfried W. Von Leibniz According to him, goodness is knowledge, and therefore if you make a mistake it is because you do not know enough. Will is the inclination to do something in proportion of the good that I know that thing contains.

We can also exploit this way of thinking of Leibniz by saying that before you form a moral opinion or say that a certain subject has done a certain thing well or badly, you have to know as much as possible, that is, the less you know, the easier it is to judge. And so his approach is intellectualistic in nature. If you perfect the intellect, you also perfect the will to want good things, and therefore according to Leibniz also happiness.

So happiness is not particularly difficult to achieve once one knows things well. This connection means that according to him there can never be indifference between two or more options, one must always choose. That is, if the intellect is properly formed, I still arrive at a choice, otherwise it means I don't know enough, so if I am indifferent I have to investigate further because no two things can exist with the same degree of virtue/goodness. Reason cannot not choose between two alternatives. We must delve deeper, otherwise ours is not a choice but an arbitrary decision.

Another statement by Leibniz is that justice is the charity of the wise person, that is, one the wiser, the more ethical. The wise person loves everyone, seeks the good. Since there is harmony among various things it is enough to understand this harmony to want to seek it.

Turning now to the Scotsman David Hume, he brings up the subject of the passions. Simplifying, the opposite of Leibniz. He says the mind is a slave to the passions, so moral distinctions come not from reason, but from moral feelings. This behavior is right means that this behavior pleases me, attracts me. We have said it before, many times we judge a thing right or wrong depending on whether we would do it, that is, we judge a subject's behavior right/wrong depending on whether that subject resembles us.

This is why there is discrimination because discrimination is often based on gender, skin color, in short outward appearance because it is easier on those things to see similarity and therefore in a subject who looks like me I find certain things more justified and condemn certain other things in a subject who does not look like me. It is a cognitive theme, that is, the moment you classify a person and think that person is bad or wrong, you will tend to remember all the wrong things they do and not see the right things. So feeling influences judgment, even in good faith, that is, when faced with the same facts, one's reading of them is very different. It is the feeling, the sensation that directs the reason.

So to say "a given behavior is right" is sometimes simply a mask for saying I like that behavior, I do it and my peers do it. The reason then I find it, so it is not reason that decides but it is the feeling that transports me and then I rationalize. It's not goodness/badness, but it's approval/disapproval, I like/dislike.

So the passions that drive moral decisions are impressions that come from outside, not ideas or reasoning, and then actions are the product of the passions. He then distinguishes between impressions of sensation, which are the clear ones (I like it, I don't like it, hot, cold, thirst, hunger, etc.) and impressions of reflection, which is what is reflected from the senses in my mind after the impression has passed.

Reason simply directs the traffic, organizes the sensations, but it is not that it drives them. So Hume rejects ethical rationalism, I am not able to decide what to do, but I am led by what attracts me and what repels me. So the opposite of the argument that we discover good and evil through reasoning, we said it at the beginning we reason and come to say what is worthy for a citizen, what is virtue, what is the good life, Aristotle, etc. here we say there is no such thing as discovering good and evil through reasoning, any action is reasonable or unreasonable depending on the premises you pose.

Is it fair to pay the arbitrators? Yes because if I don't do it others do it. So any action is reasonable in relation to the ends it produces. Reason may motivate it, but really what motivates are impulses. So gratitude is not that it is right or wrong, but it is the appropriate consequence to kindness. One does me a favor and the proper consequence is gratitude. It is not that gratitude pre-exists or is due, it is a kind of exchange. And so to act morally means to act rationally, however, it is not reason that governs the will, reason can never oppose the will, that is, it cannot derive in almost mathematical terms from reasoning, from this point of view some reason does.

Suppose we are in debt, say over-indebtedness is bad.

Suppose I say I already have too much debt, I don't want to increase it. This is rational reasoning, but does it mean I will not get into more debt? No, what matters for not getting into more debt will be the feeling of resisting making more expenses than the income I have or at least keeping a share of income over expenses to repay the debt. The same thing applies to dieting.

Most people who want to lose weight it's not that they think it's wrong to lose weight or to health it's not good for them, they just don't resist the urges enough to eat more than they need. So the problem of right and wrong is solved not at the rational level but at the level of the passions. To get to the social side, so with the passions one does what one wants, society however does not work that way otherwise it would be a bit of a mess. How do you solve it? With the concept of empathy.

Because I am governed by passions, by feeling, by sensations, I can put myself in another person's shoes and therefore I know what that person feels in that situation. And also that subject is similar to me. This is also very common, humankind is not very ethical toward animals particularly all the animals that we use many people think that they receive substantial psychological damage from the way they live, because they don't live according to nature, they don't do anything according to nature.

Going back to Hume's philosophy why does this happen? Because with a hen I personally don't find much empathy, so the fact that to make eggs she is put still, the normal hen makes fewer eggs, she hatches them, she goes around, she lives not the way we make her live but we don't have much empathy towards the hen.

Hume says we manage to be more fair to people who are more like us. This is not surprising, so much so that when you commit great crimes, great genocides, the first step is dehumanization. So many men in concentration camps are not called by their names, they are dehumanized, and that resets empathy.

So empathy will be all the greater toward my fellow human beings, the more similar they are, the more moral I am toward them. It is not an intellectual thing, it comes from empathy. So we have empathy and similarity with another subject, through this similarity we arrive at rules that we now call moral, ethical, but they are actually based on empathy.

So our judgment makes us rank people and behaviors according to how we feel and according to how close we are to that subject or subjects that resemble me.

Now let's talk about the famous Enron case. Let's look at the characters. Energy traders since they were remunerated according to the money they made, they tried to make as much money as possible.

We've already seen this with the emperor's new clothes, I mean they all do this do I have to lose my job? These subjects didn't ask so many questions because to say that they didn't know what was going to happen was a bit complicated, because one of the accusations is that at the time when there was a big demand for electricity in California (there was going to be a heat wave), these subjects brought down the power grid.

The power grid is a very complicated thing, that is, electricity can only be stored in batteries but the electricity we use is produced according to the demand that there is. So much so that when there is more demand for electricity, new power plants are turned on and when there is less, they are turned off. If it collapses, getting it going again is a mess, it takes time, so you do significant damage.

Then if there's this thing clearly the price of energy goes up, if you say tomorrow there's going to be a lot of demand because the forecast says it's going to be hot, we buy today so tomorrow we sell because it turns out that maybe there's so much demand that there's going to be a breakdown of the power grid. After that you can also produce this breakdown, for example you could phone some power plants that you own and say I see this power plant has problems, it needs to be serviced tomorrow so it should not produce power. If some people do that, the grid goes up.

So you trader up to a certain point you could be justified, in fact they were not justified. Were the traders like that because they were bad? They were conditioned by the environment, which we saw with the Stanford prison experiment and we saw with the electric shock experiment.

So the traders were made a little crazy meanwhile by the punishments, because every year every boss has to rank his employees, and those at the bottom of the rankings stay home. Another thing that happens a lot is everybody does it, or anyway if I don't do it somebody does it.

After that the other subjects are the auditing firm. Enron's business was very simple, initially it was renting pipes to bring in oil. After that it got more and more complicated, you saw it with special purpose vehicles, with energy derivatives, foreign companies, mark-to-market accounting.

The market relies on what the auditing firm says, so even the auditing firm has its faults but it would say that if it had not signed the financial statements of that company, that company would have had it signed by another auditing firm. Then you could also bring up regulation, that is, the things Enron was doing were not illegal, it was not prohibited by law to do a special-purpose vehicle.

There are companies that have interests, so they try to influence laws (lobbing). Easy to say it's wrong but more complicated is to see the whole chain of responsibility, so regulations used in a distorted way are not only a feature of Enron but also in the arms market, in the drug market, and it's also the fault of the legislature. Then there are the analysts, why were they behaving this way?

How does the relationship between society and the information world work? The analyst develops a fiduciary relationship with his readers. He is under pressure because he may want to prove that he is smarter than others. Analysts were not doing their duty but doing their short-term convenience. Then the investment banks and the audit committee.

Let's go back a bit in Greek History. Oedipus Rex, tragedy by Sophocles.

A plague rages in Thebes and Oedipus has sent Creon, brother of Jocasta, to Delphi to question the oracle. Creon then returns to Thebes bringing with him grim news: the murder of Laius still lives within the city walls.

Oedipus, who is unaware of the circumstances of Laius' death, asks Creon for clarification, who tells how the former ruler was attacked by a group of brigands on the road to Thebes. Oedipus orders the perpetrator to be found and banished from Thebes and asks Tiresias, an old blind soothsayer, to reveal the identity of the culprit. Tiresias refuses, claiming that his divination could bring even more dire consequences.

Oedipus and Tiresias clash verbally in heated tones until the soothsayer reports that Oedipus himself is the murderer being sought. Oedipus does not believe a word of what Tiresias says and begins to suspect that Creon wants to take his place on the throne, then has made arrangements with the soothsayer to drive him out of Thebes.

Oedipus then confronts Creon, who defends himself by claiming that he has no interest in betraying the king. The two men are then joined by Jocasta who, to placate Oedipus, assures him that soothsayers often give wrong answers.

As evidence of this she reports that Laius had been foretold to die at the hands of his son, whereas, as Creon has already explained to him, they had been scoundrels. Jocasta adds details, however, about the road where Laius was, and Oedipus, who recognizes that spot as the place where he killed a man and finds in the prophecy told by Jocasta echoes of the one made to him at Corinth, decides to investigate further.

Oedipus thus tells Jocasta about the prediction he received in his youth and the circumstances under which he killed a man on his way to Thebes. In the meantime, an ambassador from Corinth arrives who informs Oedipus that Polybius has died and is thus the new king of Corinth.

Oedipus, however, remembers well that the prophecy was not only about killing his father but also about incest with his mother, so he asks the ambassador what has become of her. The ambassador, however, is not just any man, but the very shepherd who so many years earlier had entrusted Laius' son to Polybius: he thus assures Oedipus that Peribea is not his natural mother. When the ambassador reports that the infant was entrusted to him by Laius' servant, Oedipus summons the old servant who still lives in Thebes. Jocasta, who has realized the deception of fate that has mocked them, tries to persuade Oedipus to abandon the need to fill gaps in the past.

But her pleas go unheeded, so Jocasta turns away and, distraught at her discovery, decides to end her life. Laius's servant, in conversation with Oedipus, recognizes the ambassador as the shepherd to whom he had entrusted the infant but is reticent to pursue the tale. Pressed by Oedipus he finally reveals that Laius had entrusted him with the infant for him to kill, but moved by pity the servant had entrusted the child to the shepherd.

Oedipus thus realizes that he is the son of both prophecies, that he killed his father and lay with his mother just as fate had decreed should be fulfilled. He then exits the scene in despair.

Oedipus, having found his mother, Jocasta, hanged dead, has used the clasps of her dress to blind himself. Oedipus then pleads with Creon, destined to become the new regent, to exile him from Thebes, as because of him the natural order has been subverted. He then greets his daughters, Antigone and Ismene, who are also destined for misfortune as they were born of a union abhorred by gods and men.

One of the most important philosophers in history was Immanuel Kant, he had a very original reasoning, it was based on the concept of duty. Back to our example of utility, is it right to torture one person to save a thousand? According to Kant, no. But not on the grounds of liberty à la Locke, that is, a person is intangible, you can't use him for any reason: this is the principle of absolute liberty (I don't have to be taxed, because life goes as it should go and I don't have to with the money I earn support someone else who does nothing).

Kant is completely different, he says it is not that you cannot touch one because you have to respect his freedom, but you cannot torture that person for yourself. Not to respect him, but to respect yourself. Which is very advanced reasoning, because he says a person's true freedom lies in doing his duty, not his pleasure. In this he reminds us a little bit of Stoicism, and that is we cannot go after our passions, because if we go after our passions we are not free.

That is, if you do something to avoid a problem, you are not respecting yourself. If a friend of yours comes with a new haircut and he looks terrible, he tells you how I look with this new haircut and you tell him, let's say if you are honest you tell him you have nice shoes.

If you're dishonest you tell him he looks good, but this you do to avoid problems for yourself according to Kant, that is you tell a lie so you don't have to have arguments, because then this one here gives you a hard time, you don't feel like putting up with it, anyway by now the hair is cut, there's nothing more to do you have to wait for it to grow back.

According to Kant this thing does not respect yourselves, not him because you yourselves have been guided by an element of comfort, by a shortcut. That is, when you are guided by some passion, and not by mere reason, you are slaves according to Kant. That is very fascinating as a thought. So duty must be done, the right things must be done not because we like it (hence hedonism, the pleasure of virtue) or even because it is convenient for us (hence I'm telling a lie because I don't feel like making it so long).

So the only true virtue is rationality, all others are subordinate to it, because even what seem like virtues to us can be used for wrong ends. For example, loyalty seems like a virtue to us, but if one is loyal to Hitler it is not a virtue. If one is loyal to a wrong system it is not a virtue. If one is loyal to the president of Enron and then takes away the electricity from the famous 200-pound lady, it is not good, that is, one is loyal to the wrong thing. The only thing to follow is reason. Paradoxically, it is only when we act in compliance with our duties that we really achieve our end and thus do the right thing. So wrong things should not be done, period.

For example, an evil person comes along and chases your son to beat him up. Your son hides under the bed. The evil one knocks on the door and says I'm looking for your son, have you seen him? You can say at most an hour ago I saw him, you are not obliged to tell him you find him under the bed, however, you cannot tell lies because otherwise you are not respecting yourself. You are using this lie to have less problems yourself, to do something that is still wrong. This thing of doing one's duty is called the categorical imperative.

The opposite is the hypothetical imperative, which means conditional, I do this thing if it suits me. According to Kant I do this thing because it is right, period. So implications should not guide us, and then what matters according to Kant is the reason, that is, if you do a right thing for the wrong reason it's still not good. So it's not enough to do a right thing, but you also have to do a right thing for the right reason: if I don't copy in the exam because otherwise I get caught, that's not good. If I don't copy because otherwise then who knows what other people think, that's not good. Because I am a slave, conditioned by other subjects.

I am really free only when I do my duty, so I don't copy because you don't copy. By obeying the rules I am truly free. You know there is a way of saying "honesty is the best policy" that is, it pays to be honest, because if you are a dishonest shopkeeper, maybe you can deceive a subject once, but then your reputation is damaged and so no one comes to you anymore. So you don't want to tell lies.

For Kant it is wrong. For Kant, telling lies is wrong, and if we want to be truly free we must do our duty without considering the consequences (hypothetical imperative, I don't do this because otherwise, or I do this because so).

Instead I do this, I don't do this because it is right, because it is wrong are categorical imperatives. Then Kant's second idea is the universalizability discourse, which is a bit like what we said about Confucius: do not do to others what you would not want done to you. According to Kant to figure out whether a law is correct or not how do you do it? So you have to do it because it is right, but how do you know whether something is right or not?

You have to see if that rule of behavior is universalizable. Is telling lies universalizable? No because if everybody told lies all the time, you wouldn't understand anything anymore.

Since you cannot universalize the practice of telling lies, then you must never tell lies. It becomes a principle so you have to abide by it all the time. Further thing is that man, your neighbor must be an end and not a means, yourself and also the other

[184]

person. You can never use yourself or others. So if you do things because you get pleasure from them, it is actually not ethical behavior. It is the opposite of Bentham, the opposite of Cyrenaics, etc.

So pleasure is wrong because if you do something, you have to do it because it's right: if you eat because you can't resist the impulse of the jar of Nutella, Nutella is commanding, not you. For Kant you must eat to nourish yourself, you must drink to hydrate yourself but you must not eat or drink for enjoyment, otherwise you are not commanding you, you are a puppet in the hands of your drives and passions. Kant's being therefore is rational and this is the principle of autonomy, that is, a subject is all the better the more autonomous it is.

A subject governed by others is not autonomous, so if I do this thing because otherwise who knows what they think of me, it is wrong. I do this thing because I understand that it is right. Innocent lies Kant does not allow them, but in society they are still allowed. For example you are a doctor and you know that a subject has a short time to live, do you have to tell him? It is controversial this, from a point of view of the principle of humanity it may well be there, for Kant it is not, the lie does not exist because it uses oneself and others.

Some commentator said that Kant's world is the realm of ends, not means, where you have to do things to realize your humanity, not for convenience or because they attract you, etc. and the end is reason.

A dramatic episode that shook Germany was the Armin Meiwes case . A case of cannibalism.

After placing an ad on a website, he was contacted in 2001 by a victim eager to be slaughtered and cannibalized. Meiwes gave him a heavy dose of alcohol and sleeping pills, mutilated his penis with a knife and tasted it in his company. Then after letting him bleed out for three hours in a bathtub, she cut his throat. After killing him Meiwes hung his corpse on a hook, dissected it, froze its flesh in a refrigerator and buried the waste in the garden, reserving the pleasure of eating it at his own discretion for 10 months. The murder might not have been discovered if Meiwes had not posted a new ad on the Internet with the intention of procuring more human flesh. Meiwes was arrested in December 2002 after an Innsbruck student phoned police after seeing new ads for more victims on the Internet. During the arrest, police officers searched Meiwes' home and found Brandes' body parts. On Jan. 30, 2004, he was sentenced in the first instance to eight years in prison on one count of involuntary manslaughter on the grounds that Brandes was consenting, while Meiwes' insanity was not recognized. Meiwes confessed to what he had done and also added the idea of writing an autobiography of his own with the aim of deterring anyone who wanted to repeat his misdeeds.

What we are interested in, apart from the affair, is the process. This was to be seen more as a kind of assisted suicide, rather than murder. This gentleman's defense is based on what principles? First of all on the principle of freedom, both of them were free, they made a contract, he explained it to them, and he explained it so well that most of them escaped, so the one there that poor guy died it's not like we can ask him, however the lawyer says surely, as the others understood the end they were going to, he must have understood it too.

He was a consenting subject, so it's not aggravated murder, because these were two free subjects who in a perfectly transparent way did something they both wanted to do: one wanted to be eaten, but it's not murder, that is, it's simply a consequence of what he does. For Kant that would not be okay because you can't use your body for things, however, if you get Kant out of the way, the principle of freedom says you're okay. One was free to get eaten and the other was free to exploit that tendency to have fun. So there is a contract, the principle of freedom is respected. The second principle is the principle of utility, that is, if the two of them like it that way, who are we to intervene? The world must be free.

The lawyer can say they didn't bother anyone, because it was something they both wanted to do, from which they both benefited. So can society interfere? But as you can see, though, it's not a story that we like so much, it doesn't come back to us so much because there are obviously higher things, so we can't just rely on freedom (everybody does what they want) or utility (everybody does what they like), but it gives us another lesson from the point of view of ethical considerations that you have to make even in finance, which is what we are interested in. It is that absolute principles do not apply, so the principle of utility is fine if one says you prefer pistachio or chocolate ice cream, however, you cannot take this principle to extremes. As well as the principle of freedom, the principle of freedom says you can't make me your slave. That's fine. But can we say, you can't ask me to contribute by paying taxes? That is, is the principle of freedom absolute? So society can never interfere/intervene?

If someone comes here and scratches me, I may not be happy. But if a guy tells me look if you let him scratch you save 100 people, I can't say no. I can't say I am inviolable and I don't even have to be scratched. I don't have to pay taxes or contribute, otherwise you go against my principle of freedom. And so the third lesson that this dramatic case gives us is that ethical principles hardly work when they are taken to extremes.

Exactly the principle of liberty does not mean that society cannot interfere in the behavior of private individuals, especially when they do not harm anyone (these gentlemen had locked themselves in the cannibal's house and for many years no one knew anything). Even the principle of utility you cannot take to extremes, so you cannot even use another person.

But Kant would also condemn the cannibal himself, because you to satisfy one of your perversions kill another person. We call it perversion, actually it is a way where you already judge, because if we want to judge it is a perversion, like eating too much or smoking too much. Who decides the limit beyond which we get to perversion? So if we don't want to judge, we say you can never intervene.

This doesn't always convince us and so we also have this additional element, which is to be careful because taking ethical cases to extremes can be useful for reasoning (as we saw with the crazy streetcar) but it is not necessarily decisive for deciding, for deciding maybe you need to have more reasoned, more moderate positions.

And in fact this gentleman was convicted. Another guy with the same kind of perversion is the Italian Marco Mariolini, who had a passion for anorexic girls. He would find them who were already somewhat anorexic, afterwards they would get engaged to him, and he would tell them that the more beautiful they were the more they slimmed down. And also to help them cope with hunger he would also beat them, and one died. So we're back to the same point again. The girl voluntarily got engaged to this gentleman, and so freedom means we cannot interfere. Then utility, we both liked the situation, he liked thinner and thinner girls, and a person who has anorexia as a psychological problem likes to get thinner and thinner.

But at a certain point there are harms that society has to deal with. So there is probably a limit to people's "free" behaviors. Our problem is: is freedom absolute? With Kant's philosophy we solve all the problems because none of these behaviors pass Kant's tests, not even victim behavior, i.e. even the victim is not innocent according to Kant because you cannot use yourself, your body to overeat (so you are gluttonous and you use food not for survival or nourishment but for other things, not for its own end but for an instrumental end) but even not eating is the same thing, you are always behaving instrumentally.

Pero precisely for the principles of utility and freedom these two cases challenge those principles.

We now focus on the English philosopher John Stuart Mill.

The principle of utility if you will, we can see it in John Stuart Mill's logic. John Stuart Mill, unlike Bentham for example or the Cyrenaics, that is those on total hedonism, said beware I am a utilitarian but utility must be a long-term utility. So in the long run even the principle of utility saves one from cannibalism, because if one spreads the fact that it is possible to eat others, it is not that one goes very far.

One needs to be a little quiet in the world so one wants rules to protect against that. So for the principle of freedom we are not saved, because either you are totally free or there is someone who intervenes and tells you how you have to live. For immediate utilitarianism okay, the long-term utilitarianism would have things to say against behavior of this kind, even toward oneself. In fact we have Mill and the focus on remote consequences: according to Mill, actions are right if they promote the overall happiness of humanity.

So Mill is also a "consequentialist" philosopher meaning a thing is good or not good if the consequences are good or not good and sometimes consequence good or not good means I like it or I don't like it. After that we have immediate consequences and remote consequences. Utilitarianism à la Bentham or the Cyrenaics says what matters is the immediate consequences, so eat a pound of Nutella.

After that Mill comes along and says but if you eat a kilo of Nutella the next day you're sick, and if you get indigestion from something or you get drunk, the next morning it's not like you have all that much of an urge to drink, and so if you've already experienced this feeling once (that the next day you're sick) maybe this thing serves you to moderate yourself earlier, so these are not immediate consequences, but they are somewhat more distant consequences. If we go on in this way we can consider the more distant consequences not only from a physical point of view (so the next day I'm sick) but also from a further point of view, from a social point of view.

So telling the lies solves the problems. Philosophers who go on virtue, who are called not consequentialists but "aretists," tell you that telling lies is wrong and therefore lies are not told. The consequentialist tells you telling lies is true that it can solve problems for you in the immediate term, however, you have to evaluate the consequences later, so if telling lies causes people to stop relying on what other people say, you haven't solved the problems.

So coming back to us, we saw the case of Enron. This issue clearly, making a false balance sheet, is prohibited. But a utilitarian would also tell you how you do it, if you make the financial statements a little bit false it's fine, so if you overvalue the assets a little bit it's fine it can happen, but if you tell too many lies then people don't believe you anymore and so the moment you go and sell your products or issue securities, people don't buy them anymore. So in utilitarian terms, even things that in the immediate you might come easy to you, you have to realize what happens later on your credibility.

So it's not that you don't tell the lie because you're honest, but you don't tell the lie because it doesn't suit you. But it's not that it doesn't suit you tomorrow, it doesn't suit you within 5-10 years. It's the famous reputation argument, we've already given the example: if I copy on the exam I'll do it sooner.

Utilitarianism one: if I get caught I get sent out, so in the immediate term it's no good, a spoonful of Nutella I'll eat, a spoonful of salt I won't. Then mediated utilitarianism: whoever sees that

I used to do all the scheming I could in college tomorrow I meet him in the workplace or someone asks for a reference about me and he says yes he's a smart guy however he's a bit of a fast learner, trying to get by. So utilitarianism at Mill is utilitarianism that is careful about remote consequences.

We take into account that utilitarianism that is very careful about very remote consequences, at a certain point it becomes virtuous behavior, because if you take into account remote consequences also in terms of humanity or in terms of the signal you give (I don't take the streetcar without paying the fare because whoever sees me gets a bad example) at that point it becomes almost bordering on virtue. So if we go further and further with the remote consequences of utilitarianism, we go toward virtue. So we say that with Mill we make the distinction between utilitarianism and hedonism. Hedonism: for our pleasure we can sacrifice other subjects. Utilitarianism à la Mill is a long-term view. However, the fact remains that according to Mill, what moves people is the consideration of utility.

After that he made another argument always in this direction. Keep in mind that Mill is a 19th century thinker and therefore more modern than Bentham. He made this kind of reasoning: there are different degrees of pleasure, that is, according to Bentham going to the theater to see Antigone is the same thing as watching a Simpsons cartoon. It is a matter of taste. According to Mill no, there are higher pleasures that involve the intellect (such as listening to classical music) and lower pleasures (such as a nice barbecue of sausage and beer). According to Bentham it is the same thing, if you like beer and sausage, I respect you the same as someone who goes to hear an opera by

[192]

Bruckner. Mill says it is better to be a dissatisfied human being than a satisfied pig. So better a dissatisfied Socrates than a satisfied fool. Clearly this is very far from pure hedonism, because you can't go and tell the fool what he likes and what he doesn't like, he has to know. In the world of utilitarianism you cannot make rankings between higher pleasures and lower pleasures, but as you see it is less consistent.

Mill in order to avoid falling into Bentham's trap whereby beer and sausage equals star chef, goes into the opposite excess, that is, he moves away from utilitarianism because it interferes with people's choice: if I like beer and sausage, what am I going to do with cilantro on a bed of lettuce? So this is Mill's utilitarianism. The example of this remote accounting Mill gives is with murder, because in terms of pure utilitarianism murder is permissible, that is, it is permissible to kill a person who does harm because humanity would benefit.

This is not such a strange argument, there are some countries even civilized countries where there is the death penalty, for example, the United States. 2-3 generations ago the death penalty was pretty much everywhere in the world. Based on what? On utilitarian calculations, i.e. to say it's better for one person to die than ten. And then there is also a signaling element, so others are more careful. According to Mill this is not usable because even if the accounting of consequences were favorable, in the case of using human life, society breaks down. Because if we respect human life, everyone is calmer and so everyone is happier, if human life is not respected, everyone is more nervous and so the overall unhappiness has to take that into account as well. So it's another way of looking at remote consequences.

How does Mill come out of this apparent contrast between utility and things that don't go along with utility? This is interesting because it is an ethical rule that could be used. Premise: Mill is writing in a time when there was no GPS, people used nautical charts to go to sea. He said that moral rules are like nautical charts, clearly you have to learn them before you go. However, when you are then at sea, the nautical chart is just a general guide, then on the individual cases you have to evaluate precisely the specific case, because maybe there is a storm or maybe there is some detour that you have to make. So this somewhat strange, somewhat moderate utilitarianism.

Finally, as far as the issue of justice is concerned, what is justice? We will see this theme of justice again later because for example in the ethical thinkers of the 20th century justice plays a big role. Mill gives justice a utilitarian foundation, saying what is injustice? Injustice is an action that when I see it, it disturbs me, it is unpleasant to me. The feeling of justice is spontaneous, and so Mill connects justice to the concept of utility. Then he adds precisely that the feeling of justice is an evolution of the feeling of revenge, so in a primordial society they do something wrong to me and I take revenge.

Since, however, it is useful to live together with others, revenge is replaced by justice, which makes me similar to others of my kind, and I try to live according to just criteria in this respect. Mill, however, does not resolve the issue of intertemporal comparison of the amount of happiness, that is, he goes completely out of Bentham's discourse in which happiness can be added up. He makes this abstract argument and moves quite far away from classical utilitarianism.

Another very important philosopher and rather complicated thinker who does not have much to do with the ethics of finance but does have quite a bit to do with ethics is Soren Kierkegaard. He reasoned in terms of 3 kinds of lives: aesthetic life, ethical life, religious life.

The aesthetic life is the Nutella life, it is concerned only with immediate pleasure, the typical figure is the Don Juan, who is not interested in sentimental relationships, one lives in the moment, etc. According to him, this way of deciding, thus immediate pleasure, does not work so much so that according to him if one is doing this life, one eventually gets bored. It's true, because there are characters in show business who end up like this, someone even commits suicide so it means that having money, being able to have fun, do drugs and do all kinds of things then in the end it's not that much fun. So the don Juan doesn't like it, because precisely one gets bored, according to him a craving is followed by despair, etc. so the life of the don Juan at some point is desperate. The ethical life is that of the family man, so he knows what is good, what is bad, he sacrifices pleasure to the achievement of good and evil.

Finally we have the religious life. The symbolic figure for Kierkegaard is Abraham, who respects the divine law and is willing even to go beyond the moral law of not killing, because if it is God who commands it, it means there is some principle of supreme justice (this was already there in philosophers like St. Thomas).

For example, Kierkegaard examines another case from Greek mythology, that of Iphigenia, Agamemnon's daughter who the gods were angry (again because of that Antigone mess) so the expedition to Troy would not succeed unless he killed his daughter. Agamemnon, because he has to obey a divine precept of the gods, kills his daughter. According to Kierkegaard there is something broader that makes you suspend human ethics, he calls it a teleological suspension of ethics that must be obeyed. For the times in which he was writing he was clearly a very countercultural subject.

Another important philosopher of the last century was British philosopher George Edward Moore.

This gentleman is interesting to us because he introduces a concept that says: it is useless for you to try to get to ethics from other things, moral judgments are objectively true or false, you don't have to look at where they come from, where they go, the consequences. This is Moore's concept of "realism." Second point he makes: we should not mess up, because ethics is a completely autonomous discipline, and we should not treat it like other categories of knowledge.

Which instead we are usually a bit tempted to do, and especially in the past the ancient philosophers had this way of reasoning that was based on doing everything, Aristotle was a full-fledged scientist, but also Spinoza, Leibniz, that is, they did the thinking men, mathematicians, physicists, whatever they could think of, and so according to Moore there are things that have to do with science (how do you calculate the area of the circle, how do you kill a calf) and things that have to do with ethics (is it right to kill a calf?) so most of the disciplines are scientific, if you do this what happens: if you tell lies people don't believe you anymore, this is not ethics this is a consequence. Ethics is: is it right to tell the lies? So either it is right or it is not right. Otherwise you are out of ethics. According to him from an epistemological point of view, that is where our knowledge of ethical laws comes from, knowledge is intuitive so it's not that we come to it by deduction from non-moral truths, because if you're in the field of science, behavior, etc. you can't go into the field of ethics.

It's something else according to him, so you can't deduce ethical principles from a world that has nothing to do with ethics. Basic moral judgments come from our intuitions, from ethical statements per se. The example he gives is this, a bit articulate, he calls it an "open question argument." Suppose there is this statement: x is good. If I say that "x is good" is equivalent to "x is pleasure" that is, I like it, from this it follows that "pleasure is good" and so if I go on it becomes "pleasure is pleasure." Then I haven't defined anything. So pleasure is a sensation, good or not good has nothing to do with sensation, because otherwise I get to the absurdity of "pleasure is pleasure." So what is good according to his reasoning remains an open question, that is, if I say something is good, it is good because it causes pleasure, then good is pleasure, then pleasure is pleasure and I have said nothing.

Of course there is the criticism of this, that this way of reasoning can translate many things into tautology. Plus it goes against the intuition that if people think that what they like is also good, you will have to take that into account a little bit. This is from a definitional point of view, from a normative point of view, i.e. what to do, Moore was an "impersonal consequentialist" what is good in impersonal consequentialism is what produces the maximum total good considering all possible people.

[197]

And so according to Moore, selfishness does not work, because to say that each person should pursue only his own good is contradictory, because if I pursue only my own good I do not go on impersonal consequentialism, because I do not take others into account. As well as the other extreme, which is the so-called "self-referential altruism" whereby one has to be concerned only about the good of those one is close to, because one has to take care of one's own good as well. So the consequentialism that he uses is a Mill-style consequentialism, indirect or layered, whereby we have to take into account the long-term consequences, just like Mill.

So Moore's is a very conservative utilitarianism, conservative in the sense that it follows rules. And what are rules according to Moore? They are what society has developed based on experience, that is what works, I have to follow social norms because that is the way I apply a second-order utilitarianism. That's what I think, but also he has some influence of Darwinism, that is, Darwin changed a little bit the way mankind thought, because until Darwin it was thought that there was some design coming from God, or nature, etc. so things exist and I have to understand why they exist. In the ancient world so the thinking was: some deity made this thing like this, look how well it works, what an intelligent person it must have been to make giraffes' necks so long. Darwin says something much simpler, he says there is no need to come up with any complicated explanation, it is simply evolution that led to this balanced situation.

Some say it can also be applied to social and psychological phenomena. And so Moore's idea of the fact that you have to abide by the rules because it is convenient, is a form of utilitarianism that comes from the consolidation of social relations, that is, it is more convenient for me to be in a society where I abide by the rules even if I sometimes get annoyed, first of all because there is this concept of utility, but then we also have to consider that we unfortunately have been selected this way, we don't like it but that's how it is.

We already don't like it if they tell us for example that the consumption of poultry in the world has increased very much after World War II, however the chickens have also changed, because until a few decades ago, before they were killed they lived much longer and weighed much less, now the weight has doubled in 2/3 of the time, this is because the chicken is a machine to turn the lowest quality feed possible into something that is in your frying pan tonight, that is, it's not that we care about the chicken. So much so that this number of days comes from the fact that they risk getting sick afterwards.

Did this thing happen? No, they were selected that way. So even the humanity we see today may have been selected this way, but not by some external entity as is the case with the chicken, simply as the chicken that doesn't get fat I don't breed it, I only breed the chickens that get fatter, psychological traits are also selected this way, the herd instinct of animals in part is innate but in part it should be selected. Because I shepherd sheep, I can't spend my time running after the ones that run away, so the ones that are very restless I let them go.

So our society is made to live in society, because hot-headed, dystonic, etc. individuals are not selected, they have a harder time moving forward, so this idea that there is a natural or non-natural evolution has changed the way of looking at things a little bit. And so even from an ethical point of view, a lot of the things that seem right or wrong to us are the things that are needed to make us live this way. It's not that somebody decided it, we decided it because we automatically expel those individuals who behave differently.

By the way, of this thing we will lose awareness because, while for the whole duration of humanity we lived in a world where there were many cultures, after that the independent cultures became smaller and smaller, i.e. anthropologists tell us that independent cultures practically no longer exist, i.e. in the world now only our Western culture is established, everyone lives more or less like that. But because the others don't work.

For example there is a culture in North America for which shame washed away with murder, because according to them if someone dies you are ashamed, when someone died even from natural causes these gentlemen go around and kill the first one they find. Clearly in New York this can't work or else everybody dies in a short time, because somebody is always somebody's somebody: somebody's relative dies of natural causes, they kill somebody else. If you're on the prairie it's different, but if you're in a city it clearly doesn't work. For these gentlemen that was the ethics, that is, that was what was expected, in their belief system that was how it worked. We don't see these things anymore, but years ago homosexuality was much less accepted and this anthropologist Ruth Benedict said look it's your problems because in ancient Greece it was widespread. It is a cultural problem, so according to her "moral" is what we call to conform to the customs of a certain society. It is the opposite of what we saw earlier with realism (good and evil exist, period).

According to Benedict good and evil is what we decide it is for the functioning of society at the moment. So each society internally decides what is acceptable and what is condemned, so morality is just a contingent relative attitude, and then if society starts to behave differently, morality evolves.

So the suspension of moral judgment only comes from cultural attitudes, which in turn are those that have evolved and allow for a given balance in a given society. Ruth Benedict also gave another interesting example, for example trans, which in some cultures is a medical problem, so forms of trans, of falling into catalepsy, but for a long time in history in various cultures it was as an example of contact with divinity. So relativism.

One particular writer who was the father of fantasy fiction was Clive Staples Levis.

According to him, morality is objective. While Ruth Benedict was completely relativist (i.e., it is moral what works in a certain culture), Lewis is an objectivist.

According to him for example just observe two people when they are arguing, these two people still come up with criteria of justice on which to argue. Like you had said it, I had behaved differently, think if someone did the same thing to you, I was there first, etc. so even those who have no study, no ethical reasoning refer anyone to a standard of behavior to which anyone expects others to conform.

By contrast he also observes that there are no cultures that value cowardice, not keeping one's word, so moral standards are objective. This is Lewis' reasoning, opposite to Ruth Benedict's. Then clearly these thinkers said many other things but we only see what we are interested in.

Then going to more modern forms of thought still we have Robert Nozick. He was a predominantly political philosopher, however we extract ethical reasoning from his political science. Sandel connects him to Locke (minimal state, liberalism, every citizen has a right to life, liberty and property, these things are intangible, you should not tax, you should not intervene in the lives of others).

According to Nozick, if there is no outside intervention, the minimal state automatically results from respecting the rights of individuals, so once we really respect individual rights, a just state would be realized. So the task of the state is to promote individual rights, so a state is all the better the more it promotes individual rights to life, liberty, property. Everything else will be done by free individuals on the basis of contracts. So according to Nozick for example our two friends from the beginning, cannibal and cannibalized, are fine.

Because if they made a contract freely it's all right. Beware that this thing of freely made contract is a topic that recurs in finance as well, so there is a rule of finance that tells us: if you want to place securities to savers, you have to inform them. Then once you inform them, they will freely decide. So the state cannot come in and say if you are a professor of finance you can buy options too, if you are a professor of philosophy you can't, because you don't know about derivatives.

That is paternalism. Liberalism says: if a person is informed, he can do whatever he wants. As usual, there is no right and wrong, because the limit of extreme paternalism is the ethical state. One of the most typical examples of the ethical state is the Nazi state, which is a very logically functioning state, too bad it was completely aberrant. It is not that we are very far in the current historical phase from the risk of ending up in such a situation, i.e., when you establish maximalisms, the risk is always that someone will come along and tell you what you can do, what you cannot do, what you must think, etc. So we have freedom (do whatever you think as long as you are informed) and paternalism. The issue of just as long as you are informed though is a very delicate one.

You hear some times "informed consent," sometimes though our consent is distorted because we are influenced by social conditions (the naked king we have seen) so you have to see very well how that consent was reached, that is, how were things represented, was the person able to understand? So beware that in a liberalist world we have the problem of consent, because we need people to make exchanges based on contracts, but contracts are based on consent and consent must be informed.

And information, apart from asymmetric information and all the things we know, is not necessarily always balanced. In fact in extreme cases it probably never is, because we are able to understand our own interests with the spoonful of Nutella but for everything else we rely on cultural systems, so if someone says to me: it's good that you study because then... I trust some experiences of others, I get ideas and I express preferences like

[203]

being here or going for a ride based on some ideas that I've received but I haven't experienced yet. So I taste Nutella, I like it, okay I have it all figured out. On other things, however, I am very conditioned, my consent is very conditioned by the society in which I live. Just think for example about the number of children per woman or the age at which you get married, these things depend on the kind of society in which you live, in some societies it is normal to get married young, in other societies it is normal to get married at an older age or never, to have one child or to have ten children.

Those who make these decisions also make them on the basis of things they do not know well. So be careful what consent is. Coming back to us, according to Nozick, freedom is either negative type: "freedom from" or positive type: "freedom to." According to Nozick, we have to entrust the state with the protection of "freedom from," no one has to bother me, I have to be free from outside interference. Whereas as for "freedom from" it is entrusted to the individual. That is, I have the right to be free from aggression, and I agree with the state producing this good for me, but I don't have the right to welfare because I can't ask others to contribute to my welfare, because otherwise I erode their freedom. If we want to use a character that is in Sandel's book, I can demand that Michael Jordan does not come and steal my drink (freedom from) but I cannot demand that he pay taxes with which I, for example, support my studies. The right to study, in Nozick's world, does not exist because it is a "freedom from." Because it means that someone pays taxes so that I am subsidized in my study, which in the utilitarian world is justified because then I pay for the studies of someone who is doing medicine and then maybe that one there in 10 years saves my life. According to Nozick this does not exist, I have to be free from aggression but not free to fulfill myself, and therefore no one has to provide services to promote me. So according to Nozick, utilitarianism to the extent that it involves sacrifices of an individual for the sake of other individuals is not good. So free trade yes, imposition no. Also according to him, private property works very well. The criticism of private property is that it tends to concentrate resources in the hands of a few, however, if there is competition and exchanges take place freely, according to him this will then benefit society as well because in an ideal capitalist world that works well, competition for resources that are one's own (you cannot take them from another, you can only exchange them) causes goods to be allocated to those who are best able to value them. That is, imagine that I run a bar where I make $1,000 a day in takings, have a certain customer base, etc. This bar is valued at a certain amount. If someone comes in and offers me more than the amount at which I value it, and then he instead of making $1,000 a day in takings makes $5,000 the economic system according to Nozick improves, because he is better than me since he can get more customers. This is something that happens all the time. In Piazza Cordusio in Milan (Italy) there used to be a post office, where one could go to buy stamps, mail, etc. how much could such a world make?

Not very much. Along comes someone who puts in a coffee chain, earns much more and can pay much more rent than the post office. And in this case both of them are happy, maybe all three considering the property owner. The post office is happy because somebody paid them to go away, Starbucks is happy because they make a lot of money, the property owner is happy because he doubled the rent.

All because of freedom. If we on the other hand had made a law where we said that because there traditionally are post offices there, there are the old ladies who are used to picking up their pensions there, it's not fair, etc. in this way we interfere with freedom and the economic system is harmed or otherwise not promoted. So freedom encourages competition for the competitive use of resources. Also according to him, since there is private property, people are in favor of making long-term contracts and thus the system improves.

Especially from a philosophical point of view, this kind of private property, etc. is closer to the natural state. Many philosophers talk about the state of nature, the state that would be realized without human intervention. This question of the state of nature has been variously criticized because when we think of the state of nature, we think of the state of nature but we evaluate it with our eyes of now. Coming to my usual metaphor of chickens, it's like the chicken that thinks, how nice it would be to be free and fly, but the problem is that you don't know if you are able to fly, according to your evolution. So you can't think about what the state of nature is with the eyes of now, with the criteria of behavior now modified by life in civilization. And anyway according to him, who does not have this criticism, he says freedom is the closest thing to the state of nature, that is, the state in which there is no intervention from outside. Clearly this is a principle that does not go along with the Kantian idea that everyone must be treated as an end, not a means.

Another criticism is that it does not consider that my intangibility is not really so much mine. For example, I am the great soccer player or basketball player and I say you don't have to tax me, I don't want to take care of society because I am the one who is good, I am the one who trains even when I am injured. And I say, you are very good, however, all the money you have comes from where?

From you or from the fact that there is a society that buys the jerseys the jerseys, the underwear, comes in 40,000 to the stadium, I mean it's all yours? If you were alone in the state of nature that you claim to have, you would not be like this. So is the credit all yours or is it partly also the world around you? Mainly because your talent is not that it is yours, it is a fluke.

Another example that always has to do with soccer is the Insigne brothers. There are 3 Insigne brothers who play soccer, the strong one is Lorenzo, then there is one who is a little bit less strong, and then there is Antonio who is the poorer one. Same family, same genes, same everything, they probably even went to the same school, one makes millions and the other will make $600 a month.

Who can the lesser brother blame? No one. It's not that he can say eh though I could have been born in another family or in another period, that is if Lorenzo had been born in the 1500s when soccer was not played, maybe he was a shoemaker. Which was the talk of: whose credit is it?

These here same family, same everything, one plays in minor leagues and one plays in the national team. What merit does the one who plays in the national team have? Practically none, I mean I don't see any differences really his. It's a fluke, due to the fact that he's probably a little bit faster, maybe he's even shorter, he's a little bit more agile, he's a little bit more such that he's playing in the top league and making a lot of money. Yay.

This is to say that when we go to see what is merit we have to be very careful because if you talk to him he says: I have been running after a ball since I was 5 years old, etc. but also his brothers. What is merit? If the merit is mine, nobody can touch me, Nozick. But if the credit is not so much mine, it's a case, some of it comes from society because there's no law that says soccer players have to be paid more than field hockey players.

Clearly the soccer player says yes but the one who goes to the curling Olympics is the best among the 1,000 who play curling in the U.S., I am the best among the 3 million who play soccer in the U.S. so if you allow there is a big difference. Another one says yes however if one day curling becomes fashionable, the sides will be reversed. And is it up to you? No, it is not something you can control, but it is a society thing. Also, the talent is not that you won it, you found it. It's a fluke, so the inaggredibility of what I have, which is very well justified if I acquired it or deserved it, less justified in a world where I stole it, of course, but also found it for myself.

And many things have to do with that, that is, they have to do with external circumstances or issues that we don't control.

For example, natural resources, I mean it's not that there's any particular merit to owning a piece of land in New York, because 300-400 years ago it probably wasn't worth anything, so much so that if you go and see New York it belonged to the Dutch who sold it for cheap. After that it developed later because it was in the right place. It was a place that was quite close to Europe, and so at the beginning of the century for trade the crossing ended there, but it's a fluke. So where is the credit?

Natural resources belong to everybody, some might say, they are not yours because you didn't deserve them. And then there is another issue. The United States initially belonged to England. The basic ideology of westward expansion in America was: the moment I clear a land that is nobody's, so I come to a certain place, clean it up, plant tomatoes, etc. if somebody comes and takes my tomatoes I get angry and shoot them (Locke's idea). The reasoning is that no one can come and touch something that you have fenced and cleared because it took you time to do it. If someone comes and takes tomatoes it is like saying be my slave for 1 day, 2 days, 3 days, 1 month. Because we don't like this thing even private property must be protected because you have mixed yourself through your work with the land. And this is also said by Nozick, one criticism is that the reverse is also true. The moment you mix your work, so you mix a thing that is yours, time, with a thing that is not yours, that is nobody's or is somebody else's, what happens? One might say but this reasoning is stupid because it can be reversed, that is, you having mixed your labor with the land, you have lost the ownership of your labor, because who is it that said someone else did not own the land? It is just because you have the rifle and the other one does not, from a material point of view the opposite can also be valid as a philosophical argument. So Nozick gives us this modern liberalism: minimal state and minimal interference.

Another very interesting philosopher is Rawls, also a contemporary. The reasoning until Rawls was: freedom, utility, etc. but to make contracts you need consent, that is, without consent you cannot have moral obligations. Earlier we talked about informed consent which is also there in medical disciplines, for any medical practice you sign informed consent. In the medicine sheets sometimes at the end there is the word death, in some cases you die and one clearly is not taking the pill to die. Is that informed consent? Or is it the pharmaceutical company or the hospital protecting itself from liability? How informed is this consent? To make a truly informed consent you would have to be a doctor who is familiar with that drug, etc. so even consent is overstated. We have said this before. Rawls takes it a step further and talks about "presumed consent." Presumed consent is that: a thing you may or may not do ethically if that thing would be agreed upon even by a person who doesn't know where he stands in the transaction. What is this for? This serves because when you reason about: this thing is right or this thing is not right, very often you put yourself in someone's shoes.

For example, taken from the world of finance as usual, there is a law that says: there must be a minimum of the least represented gender on the boards of listed companies, the so-called pink quotas. Is that fair or not? Typically for women it is considered fair, men who lose their board seats consider it not fair (of course they don't say why do I lose my seat, but they say eh but actually if I would also consider experience, by definition one who is there is more experienced than one who comes in and so if you take experience into consideration this game is lost).

A person tends to judge based on their situation, so typically a woman will tend to consider this more fair and a man maybe tends to consider it less fair than a woman does. Because each of us, in judging various situations, cannot get away from our own situation. Think of all the debates about immigration, etc., even the most thought-evolved people have a hard time breaking out of their character, because there is nothing to be done, our mind, our mental categories are daughters of the experience we have had up to that point. Whether we realize it or not, so these arguments that we make with the ethics of finance are really to say: well I understand how I think, let's try to see if with the help of some ideas received from some philosophers you can see it differently as well.

So Rawls says: be careful that you every time you judge you start from an assumption, which is your situation. To understand properly you should put yourself behind the veil of ignorance, and that is not knowing whether you are a man or a woman, young or old, rich or poor, unemployed or not, immigrant or not.

The veil of ignorance is Rawls' most important finding in deciding what is the best solution. And so the best solution in the case of a moral dilemma is the decision that an informed person would make, but without actually knowing where he stands, who he is. Keep in mind that any regulation like pink quotas does injustices. Imagine you are in the bachelor's degree at this university and you want to enroll me in the master's degree. You make a nice rule that says we take 30 percent from other universities: right, wrong, who knows?

Because those who would be out of 100 from place 71 down say to me it's not that I'm so convinced by this rule because I've been here, I've done 3 years here, I expect to go on here. Whereas those who are out say it is fair to give the opportunity to those who want to specialize, to get in.

So what is fair and what is not fair depends on what point of view you see it from. Or you have to use average as a criterion or you have to use a chronological criterion, whatever criterion you use somebody gets in and somebody gets out. The criterion has to be such that it is acceptable to both sides, because if you reason according to your situation (that you would be in or you would be out) you are affected by this issue.

So it is the criterion of the person who does not know what position he or she is in. Obviously this way of reasoning doesn't apply to everything, clearly it's not Kantian, there's a background of utilitarianism in this because at that point one says if by sacrificing one person you save 1 million, at this point we have to sacrifice them. There is a kind of advantage/disadvantage accounting in this approach, according to Kant this you cannot do. In fact Rawls says be careful, because this contractualism and this cooperation is not that it can go beyond certain limits.

And what are those limits? The fundamental freedoms. So you can't erode life, freedom of speech, freedom of religious belief, that comes first. Having said that, do you have to promote equality? No, you don't have to promote equality, but you can tolerate those inequalities that bring comparatively greater benefits and that would be decided by any party without knowing where they stand.

So if you go and ask Bezos (Amazon) , who is one of the richest people in the world, whether it is fair to pay taxes he says no, because I can pay for everything I need. I can pay for my hospital, police, judges so I don't need the courts, I defend myself with bodyguards, I travel with the helicopter that is mine. He doesn't need the others, however if he reasons in terms that he is not necessarily in that condition, he might also say well sure some tax can also be paid because you never know where you stand.

So inequalities are allowed, but only to the extent that it benefits those who are currently disadvantaged and that anyone would judge fair without knowing which side they are on.

And then he says another thing also applied in finance, with some restraint due to the fact that usually in society the strongest individuals get stronger and stronger. This thing in finance is applied in the weak contractor rule, that is if you go to the bank to underwrite a certain financial product, for example in many situations there is a reversal of the burden of proof. The burden of proof is that if I say, he owes me $100, it is I who has to prove that he owes me $100, not he who has to prove that he does not owe me $100.

The person who makes an objection has to prove it. Again, we are moving away from this, that is, the moment there are political ideas that say: you have to prove you are not corrupt, actually there is someone who has to prove that I am corrupt. If you underwrite a financial product, you think the bank has harmed you and you complain, it is the bank that has to prove that it did not sell you the wrong product, it is not you who has to prove that the product is wrong.

Why is this in a Rawls world? Because power tends to accumulate. The second thing is that unfortunately in societies as they are made the rules are decided by the fittest, who have many ways of influencing the rules that are made, and so it is good that there may be some corrective in favor of the weaker, even if you don't know which side you are going to be on. Rawls' last idea is the following, which we have already seen when we talked about egalitarianism.

As a general idea we like equality, it is a right idea, we are all equal. The problem is that we are not all equal, that is, the only way to make Antonio Insigne (a mediocre soccer player) score as many goals as Lorenzo Insigne (one of the best players in the world), is not to make Lorenzo Insigne play. So you cannot make the weakest equal the strongest in any other way than by handicapping the strongest. But that doesn't suit the club.

Think about it in the economic situation, you say it's not fair for the CEO to get 20 times what the employee gets. But if the CEO gets 20 times what the employee gets because he makes, like Lorenzo Insigne, win his team, either you reduce how much you pay him but it's not like you can say to the employee I'll pay you the same as him because he's not capable anyway, he can't make it.

That's true in any field, I mean people unfortunately are different, even by a little bit but maybe it's that difference that makes the difference. So if you don't like inequality, and there are very good reasons why you don't like inequality, you can't make people equal except by handicapping the best.

So if you can't handicap the best to make them more like the disadvantaged, what Rawls proposes is the so-called "difference principle." So you can't make people equal because it doesn't suit you, the only way would be to make Lorenzo Insigne play with a 20-pound backpack on him, at which point he becomes as strong as his brother. Does it suit anyone though?

No because in Italian Serie A neither of them plays. The principle of difference is that inequalities are allowed only if, in the unequal world, in the let's call it unjust world the unfortunate are better off than the alternative condition.

The father of the Insigne brothers might say, my sons must all be equal, so let's have Lorenzo play with a 20-pound backpack, the one who plays a little better with a 10-pound backpack and the other without a backpack, so we make them all equal. Or we can say, dear children everyone follows his talent and does what he wants however please dear Lorenzo, you pay for the vacation home.

So the brother who gets $600 a month can have either $600 a month and not the vacation home in the good place or $600 a month and the vacation home in the good place, because even if he cripples Lorenzo anyway, he still gets $600 a month.

So if we get out of the football metaphor, inequalities are allowed but only if, in the relationship between two situations with different inequalities, the disadvantaged are better off. So we have the talent handicap situation: with the 20-pound backpack, but nobody needs it.

The Nozick situation: don't get involved, whoever is better is better, whoever is not better is his own damn business, or the

Rawls situation: freedom to talents, but with the condition that the disadvantaged have a better situation.

Because according to Rawls you don't know where you will be and so it is true that if you were the very good one you would like to be, but since you don't know you are better off in a situation where everyone is free but someone provides something compared to the ungoverned situation or where we all get $600 a month and nobody goes on vacation. Taking into account that talents are assigned by chance, that they are not ours, which we often forget.

According to Rawls, among the things that we receive is also the structure of society, so the political constitution, the legal system, the economy, etc. we can't say is based on a consensus system, because none of us gave consent to where we are born. But at the same time it is not that we are so free to go elsewhere. We are not completely not free, but it's not that we are so free to change the system, to go somewhere we maybe like better. So even institutions are a given thing for us and have a profound effect, just think of education.

Next lecture we will look at Habermas and MacIntyre, who introduce a very important new topic, which is what is called "discourse ethics," and that is that many of our decisions about right and wrong are based on how we tell the story. So we are not presented with an absolute ethical dilemma, it's not like someone catapults us to Mars and asks us what you would do. We are children of our experience and also of how we tell ourselves about it. What in times past was the narrative, synonymous with manipulation. So think about what your decisions depend on how you represent them in your head, the words you use or when you see something try to think about how they affect how you then decide the ways things are told/represented.

Another interesting philosopher is Jugen Habermas.

He is one of two philosophers interested in discourse ethics. Habermas says a certain rule in order to understand whether it is moral, those to whom that rule applies must have had the opportunity to debate and judge it consciously. That is, he does not say "you must decide," but he says "you must debate it and consensus must form." In all of these cases you create a moral case, we've seen it with Oedipus Rex as well, the problem with Greek tragedy is that everybody is right from their point of view, that is, there is a conflict. So whenever you have to decide whether something is right or wrong it means you are enduring a conflict. Then Habermas says since conflict is ineradicable (but you have to develop a rule because otherwise things don't move forward, if you never agree it's worse for everyone) you have to develop those rules that have been subjected to a debate in which everyone has been able to participate.

Not "has participated" but "has been able to participate" meaning if you don't have anything to say you can just shut up. So everyone who is affected by a certain rule should have a chance to participate in the discussion. Debating one's opinion does not mean simply saying it, but also having arguments. Debate must be open, everyone's contributions must be treated with equal respect, one must bring evidence to support one's argument, one cannot impose rules without otivation, but neither can one reject them without debating them. And so the ethical rule is not just about a problem of "is it good or not?" but it is also a problem of how it was developed and whether it was debated.

This is discourse ethics so we justify theories that have been subjected to an articulate debate in which everyone has been able to participate and has participated genuinely, that is, by submitting their ideas to public debate. This according to Habermas is the real task of democracy.

Then if you like, it is a world that tends to develop elites, because if there is a person who has a strong moral sense but is not good at speaking, his ideas will be represented less, and vice versa, if a person is good at speaking but has poor ideas, these will be represented in a way that makes them fascinating. So Habermas' theory does not apply to direct democracy, where one jumps up and if he is better at influencing the masses than the others he prevails, it applies to representative democracy, where as a result of debate, consensus is formed. Since everyone is equal in a parliament, it is difficult for one to mislead the other. On the other hand, if I put a prepared person in a debate with people who are not highly prepared, it easily manipulates them, leads them to make considerations that seem like reasoning but are not. So in a society with representative democracy, in a debate among peers Habermas' rule works, that is, rules are applied only after there has been an opportunity to debate them among informed people. Rules have to be debated because there is no absolute rule beyond a few basic rules such as don't kill, which is why debate is necessary.

On the topic of discourse we find another important philosopher, MacIntyre. According to MacIntyre what matters is what we tell ourselves, what matters is narrative identity. Again with the discourse of conflict, a conflict we have already seen but have not dealt with is Antigone. In this tragedy the conflict lies in the fact that each character has his own reasons if we see the story from his point of view (even Creon). Basically according to MacIntyre the argument depends a lot on how you tell it. Kant for example would be on Creon's side because the law must be obeyed anyway if it is our duty. Utilitarians would say if we allow someone to stop obeying a law, then no one obeys it. MacIntyre says our ethical choices apparently are abstract, but we actually belong to something: we belong to a certain age group, to a certain geographical area. Given that there is this issue of identification and belonging, are we really free to decide what is right and not right, or are we conditioned by belonging? MacIntyre says that we are conditioned. Think about the sense of belonging to a nation. This again creates a conflict, because there are levers of belonging, but in some contexts they are not legal (e.g., the professor cannot let some students copy just because they support the same soccer team as him). ! Beware that the obligation to belong is a bit strange, because it is not an obligation I contracted but it happened. In Sandel's book for example, it talks about the fact that the Greeks want compensation from Germany for the damages of World War II, but the Germans, who had nothing to do with the war or the exterminations, do not agree. It is the same case with Americans who have to compensate the oppressed Native American community with taxes. Where does belonging come from? From the stories we tell ourselves. Our life is not something that happens, but it is something we tell ourselves and tell others. According to MacIntyre, good is something that goes in the direction of my story, evil is something that subverts in a way that I don't like the direction of my story. So in the same situation, what changes is how we tell it. As we live and form an identity (or does some-one form an identity for us?) our decisions we make stem from consistency with the story we tell ourselves.

Many decisions about what one does or does not do depend very much on habit, on belonging: my decisions feed my story. So for MacIntyre, abstract principles (such as utilitarianism, freedom, good life) are not enough, but much depends on past behavior that determines a trajectory for me relative to future behavior.

Beyond Antigone there is another very interesting story in Sandel's book, that of General Robert Lee. He was a Virginian general who fought in the War of Secession. Virginia was among the states that rebelled. Note that Lee's family had always been very powerful, and he was not among the secession hotheads, i.e., he would have survived quietly even with the new laws. Lee despite this, resigned his commission with the regular army because he could never raise a weapon against his relatives/citizens. Other military personnel in the same state did not do what Lee did. This shows that both the bonds of belonging and how we tell ourselves things matter.

One of the recent philosophers we analyze is Ronald Dworkin.

Dworkin says we are responsible for the choices we make, yet our choices are "fitted" to a set of characteristics, let's call them "natural endowments" that are arbitrary, that is, they are innate, not earned. Natural endowments are intelligence, likability, work ability, health. However, there are profiles that are rewarded by society. Just think of what has happened with mass communication, some famous people today probably would have been nobody 200 years ago. Dworkin develops a notion of "ethical liberalism," saying that we need the same ground rules for everyone.

Then equality is not access to resources by everyone equally, that is, it is not in terms of outcomes, we don't all have to have the same goods but equality is always in terms of opportunity. Since the good is something that someone wants, if one person takes it, another person cannot take it. And so in the face of any distribution of goods, any criteria benefits someone to disadvantage someone else. Dworkin is quite "secular" with respect to things in the face of which we express a relevant preference. For example in the case of parents who "bought" their children's admission to prestigious U.S. universities, Dworkin would say that it is a legitimate thing to do, because nowhere does it say that the selection criterion must stipulate that only deserving students are admitted, or 10 percent must be foreigners, etc.

According to Dworkin the rules are all on the same level, what matters is that you use a selection criterion that is consistent with the mission of the selecting party. So if I want to send a message that I want to have people from many parts of the world, then I'm going to reserve in the next call for undergraduate admission a few places for internal candidates. Clearly the internal applicants will say that's not fair. Actually according to Dworkin this is not a problem, it depends on the goal the institution has, if the institution wants to increase diversity because it believes it benefits everyone, it can do so. Dworkin gives an example that occurred at the University of Austin in Texas, whereby black students were not admitted. The same argument can be made for pink quotas. Ethical liberalism: anything that meets the purpose of the deciding institution is fine. So two things:

merit does not exist, or rather it is a much-told thing. It's no one's merit that society at this moment in history values soccer players more and in others musicians, etc. The fact that that characteristic is valued by society does not depend on the individual.

The one who has to set the selection criteria is not the selected, but the one who has to select, even though we may not like it. Some discrimination is accepted, if justified (for example, a person without a hand cannot drive a bus). This has costs in terms of inequality, and if we go too far we arrive at a caste system. The recipient decides the rule, not the stakeholder.

Most famous and always debated was Friedrich Nietsche.

For Nietzsche, there is no morality; his most famous phrase is "God is dead." Everyone does what he wants, the strongest prevails. Our values do not come from outside, there is no God, nature or something outside of us that determines what is right and what is wrong and we must conform. We are responsible. Christian piety according to him is a herd feeling, harnessing weak people. But the strong person, the real man has no rules, because he makes them.

What he makes is the law. And so our background determines us, we struggle to control ourselves, however, the good is not given. Our evaluation of good and bad very often depends on agreeableness/unpleasantness: we judge something as good or bad based on present or imagined agreeableness/unpleasantness. If we imagine putting our hand on fire, it is unpalatable to us even if we do not. So physiological instincts unconsciously guide our choices, much of the good and not good comes from these things, which determine us.

We think we have mastery over our thoughts, in fact these are largely autonomous from us. Our behavior, our morality is a chemical, biological thing (even if he was not a follower of Darwin he comes to much the same conclusions). In behavior, certain things have been affirmed not because they are right or wrong, but because they serve the purpose of coexistence (e.g. monogamy: the evolution of mankind made it affirmed, so that society progressed). Similarly, for Nietzsche, the moral rules we have are conditioned by evolution; they are the things that were needed. So justice, prudence, moderation, courage in short the Socratic virtues are actually animal virtues, they only serve to improve the efficiency of living together. For example, being polite serves to make our lives easier: we do not behave well because of a moral argument, but because we can live together better. Every so often then according to Nietzsche precisely the man who breaks the mold pops up. Even altruism according to him is a mystification, that is, we have been educated to feel good when we do something altruistic, but in reality it would not be in our best interest. The truly free subject is the one who stands beyond good and evil. Laws are constraints, walls. The superman breaks conventions and creates a new "moral" system.

An important living philosopher is Peter Singer.

Balancing interests between human beings, so not equal treatment but equal consideration of interests. It is the concept of marginal utility. Singer says that the interest of a hungry subject, for the same amount of food, must outweigh the interest of a satiated subject, because the marginal utility of the hungry subject is greater. So his thinking has utilitarian characteristics, and therefore the most important interests are to satisfy basic needs and to avoid pains, with an idea of universalization. Singer makes a strong criticism of Kant on the issue of universalization. According to Singer, Kant in his universalization forgot about animals. For example we might think that the total amount of human happiness has on average increased, fewer people die of hunger/disease, etc. but at the cost of what could we say? If we put animals in the account probably the balance is not the same, because animals live much worse now than a hundred years ago and are exploited (especially farm animals, industrially exploited). If we look at the overall suffering of living beings this has increased, even though humans live better. Singer then makes this critique of Kant's universalizability by saying that it has the limitation of not considering animals. So according to Singer we need to go to an idea he calls "effective altruism," that is, we should not just try to reduce suffering, but we should reduce it in the most effective way possible (reduce poverty and the suffering of everyone, including animals).

Singer's for example is the analogy of the child drowning in the pond: if while walking we see a child drowning in the pond, we will surely try to save him. If in our haste we forget the cell phone in our pocket, we lose €500 of the phone, but we have saved a life. Singer says place this, why then will we be more reticent to do charity to help someone who is dying? Take $500 and wire it to a child in Africa who is dying. Still on the subject of animals, Singer says that we often consider creatures that are not very similar to each other and very different from us creatures that "look like us."

Berlin says all human problems can be solved through an appropriate method, usually reason. And so evil, bad things are daughters of ignorance, of not understanding what is good. Human nature, however, is not fixed, in the sense that there is no list of characteristics. Characteristics can vary from individual to individual, from culture to culture. The philosophers seen earlier had as difference from these in the fact that they did not travel, St. Thomas it is not that he could think that there were other ways of living. Characteristics may vary, but with limits. Berlin makes the metaphor of the human face. The human face can change depending on the geographical area, the eyes can be more or less slanted, the nose can be made a certain way, etc. however, it always remains very easily recognizable as human. So a kind of "objective pluralism" so many objective values but different ways of declining them, just like the human face. And objective values can be identified by our instincts, our natural feelings. So seeing a subject suffering injustice or rather what we think is injustice, makes us feel bad and this thing according to him is quite innate. After that, the various cultures have changed, so there is pluralism but there is this underlying ethic. There are many genuine values, however, they can come into conflict. If you remember this we have already seen this in Aristotle, on gradation. For example, freedom can conflict with law and order or equality, piety can conflict with justice (as in

Antigone, who out of piety creates injustice), then love can conflict with impartiality and fairness, knowledge with happiness (think of Oedipus), etc.

Thomas Nagel, a contemporary American philosopher, speaks of "moral luck." Kant said that what matters are intentions. The problem is that if we put chance, or let's call it luck, in the field, how do we make moral, correct judgments? That is, it would behoove everyone to be morally judgmental about the things they control. For example if one bumps into you or if one throws water on your computer keyboard, one might say but can't you be more careful? But if the water on the computer keyboard gets there because it was in turn bumped by another person, or because a meteorite fell, you don't get angry in the same way. That is, everyone is held morally responsible for the things that are under their control, let's call it the "principle of control." So if a person on the subway steps on my foot, I can say but can't you be careful? If this happens because the train had sudden braking, there was nothing he could do about it. This principle of control we put it together with Kant's argument, and that is what matters is intentions. So if I do something for the wrong reason, I do an ethically wrong action. For example, if I am honest not because I have to be honest, but because it is convenient for me to be seen as honest, then it is not good. Imagine getting a job where there is a probationary period: I behave well for that period, then I get hired on a permanent basis and start slacking off. If I behaved well not because in my opinion that's the way to work, but only to make it to the end of the probationary period, I have deceived my counterpart and therefore morally I have done a wrong thing. So motives matter.

According to Nagel, the Kantian idea is important, however, he adds the following question: what role does luck play in this? So it is true that we are morally assessable depending on our intentions, depending on what is in our control, however, two people who want to do the same thing (same intention) but do a different thing by an accident of luck, are they judged differently? There are two drivers who are the same, i.e., they have taken the eye test, they are both cautious, neither of them has been drunk, they take the same road, the problem is that on that road when one passes, nothing happens, when the other passes, a dog that has escaped from its owner's control crosses the road and is run over by the car. Do the two drivers have different responsibilities? Normally we would be inclined to say yes, that is, the owner of the dog takes it out on the person who ran over his dog. However, if we consider this abstract Kantian world, in which we introduce the combinations of chance, we get a doubt because the moral responsibility of both is equal; unfortunately, chance wanted this to happen to one and the other did not. Beware many times we judge a person's ethics according to the actual consequences. According to Kant this should not happen, so attempted murder and murder, for Kant should be the same thing. If I want to kill a person, in one case I succeed, in another case for a combination of events I don't succeed, the gun jams. I didn't have different intentions, though. In the penal code murder and attempted murder have different penalties, theft and attempted theft have different penalties but the person's intention is the same in both cases, simply the circumstances made the outcome in the end different. So moral luck conditions our judgment, when we judge we also have to see if we take too much into account the consequences, and how much of those consequences are due to bad luck or luck. According to Nagel there are four kinds of impact of luck on ethics:

1) resulting (or consequential) luck, which is luck as it goes: two murderers plan the same murder, then by chance one achieves his goal and is therefore guilty, the other by chance does not achieve his goal and is therefore not guilty. But they both have exactly the same intentions. How much is one responsible for consequences and how much responsible for intentions? An example that is given when talking about intentions and results is that of the painter Gauguin: at one point he drops everything in France and moves to Polynesia, he does not do it to achieve goals, however, he becomes a great painter. Did he foresee this? Probably not, and so this is an example of what combinations can give. So do we condemn him because he abandoned his family or are we happy because we had a great painter? Are we going to judge him differently depending on the outcome? If he had gone to Polynesia and devoted himself to drinking rum, would we judge him differently? So how much does chance affect? This is the resulting luck, we judge whether something is good or not depending on the result it produces, but beyond the person's intentions. We always have to be careful about that. It also applies in the world of finance, until Enron went bankrupt the way it was run was fine, they thought they were bad, however they produced good results. Some things are seen as bad when they start to go bad, as long as they go well they are tolerated. Often things that look bad are tolerated because they produce good results and vice versa.

2) Substantial luck, which is luck resulting from the circumstances in which I find myself. The example Nagel gives is that

in Nazi Germany a lot of people were guilty of crazy crimes, but because they were in a certain environment, and he says if a lot of those people in 1929 had emigrated to Argentina, maybe they would have become quiet businessmen. They were going about their lives, they were not in that environment. So how much did the case affect their moral responsibility? It doesn't mean justify, but it means how much did the case affect it? This obviously applies in many cases of deviance, that is, if one grows up in a degraded environment what is his responsibility in the wrong things he does or vice versa if one grows up in a positive environment what is his merit in the fact that he behaves in a certain way? In many cases people did not oppose it, they could have raised their hand and said this thing is wrong, I must not do it. It's true of Nazism and it's true of Enron, so how much does the environment affect people's behavior?

3) constitutive luck, what responsibility does a subject have for being made a certain way? Who we are is not entirely up to us, we don't necessarily have all this choice, there are those who can be braver, less brave. For example, there are people who suffer from vertigo and people who do not suffer from vertigo. It is very difficult for a person who suffers from vertigo to induce him not to suffer from vertigo, that is, to explain to him that he should not suffer from vertigo or many other personal characteristics. So if one subject is less brave than another, is it a moral characteristic or is it a constitutive characteristic? Imagine the example of the child who falls into the pond, one jumps in to save him, another does not because he is fearful. Or a person is attacked on the street, one person intervenes to help and another does not. Because maybe one is braver and the other is less brave. Did one do right and the other did wrong?

Yes, but how much did personal characteristics affect it? Courage can be a bit like vertigo. Very often the environment also influences us in such a way that we cannot clearly decide, and so here again, what behaviors am I ethically responsible for since so many out-of-control things affect me?

4) random luck that depends on previous circumstances, i.e., I am in a certain situation because there was something else before and so I am in a certain situation by chance, I may not have freely chosen certain situations. And so chance influences. The general lesson of this talk by Nagel is that when we judge an ethical situation, we must also ask ourselves what role chance played. Clearly we can also go to the extreme and say everything is chance, so there is no fault. The other extreme case is nothing is chance, everything is the responsibility of the subject. Of course, the solution is usually intermediate.

Summary

The first thing we have seen is that ethical reasoning is different from other kinds of reasoning. If we reason on the basis of what we have seen we can imagine that we have had three periods: the ancient period before Christianity, then a long period occupied by Christianity, and then from the Enlightenment onward there has been increasing rationalism. It is a fact, however, that even if we read ancient texts by Aristotle or Socrates we do not find wrong reasoning, sometimes it is affected by the era in which it was made. For example, until Darwin, it was thought that the various things that existed were made in a certain way because that is the way it had to be. Aristotle thought there was a nature of things. The nature of the flute is to make a good sound, and so you have to give to play the flute to people who are capable of extracting the best sounds. The nature of a tree is that if it is in good condition it develops in a certain way, of course if something happens to it like a fire or a drought it will not reach its full nature, however, there is this concept. This was in the ancient philosophers. In Christianity even more so, because there is a creator who made things in a certain way, being good he made them right and orderly. After that, we have the last stage, which we can summarize by Darwin, who says that things are the way they are because they evolved that way because in natural selection a certain situation was created. If the lion was not so fast it would starve to death. The slow lions died and the genes that were passed on were those of the faster lions. So according to Darwin we only have to take into account that certain characteristics are established. These are the great stages of thinking, however, we did not happen to have something completely absurd in the things we saw. In the natural sciences, there is an evolution, for example, Aristotelian physics was completely overtaken by Newton. Aristotelian physics was based on the fact that things must stand still, there must be something that sets them in motion. In contrast, Newton's physics was based on the fact that things are in the state they are in, so if they are moving they will continue to move, if they are stationary they will remain stationary.

Later Newton's physics was completely superseded by Einstein's physics. So while with some natural sciences it is possible to scientifically prove the superiority of one approach over another, in ethics it is not so, that is, it is impossible to prove the superiority of one approach over another, and then there are no so-called "ethical facts." Facts are human, however, there is no moral fact, right or wrong are reasoning, it is not a quantity that I can measure. Last aspect is that the same ethical norm in some situations works, in others it does not, in some societies it is accepted and in others it is not. For example in the Greek world, Aristotle was perfectly comfortable with pedophilia and slavery, which in today's world would create more of a problem. So ethical inquiry often does not lead to conclusive results because it cannot be proven, because there are no ethical facts, and because ethics changes over space and time. Getting pregnant before marriage years ago was seen as a problem from a social point of view; today it is no longer. Another example that is given to demonstrate the difference between ethics and other sciences is the case of abortion. From the medical point of view it is a very uncontroversial topic, that is, the practices that lead to the termination of pregnancy are not debated, on the other hand whether it is right or not can be the subject of endless debate, when you start life, whether the fetus has rights, etc. so it is very easy from a medical point of view, very complicated and unsolvable in definitive terms from an ethical point of view. Another thing seen in some reasoning but which we have never defined in this way is the "naturalistic fallacy," that is, very often in ethical inquiry, especially in the past, we derived from what is what ought to be. This was a problem. Because there are slaves it is right that there should be slavery, Aristotle said. Because there are jobs that slaves do, they serve and therefore slavery is needed. After that I also see that slaves don't run away, that they don't kill the master even if they could, so it means that they are okay with that too, they have a slave nature, they are children of slaves and it's okay for them to be slaves. We don't really like that as reasoning however, the reasoning was exactly that. The mistake was to draw from things that are the way things should be, and this is true even in modern society. The status of women, the status of immigrants, etc. from a thing that is if you are not very careful you draw conclusions about how that thing must be. If one buys certain securities one can lose money, you know, and so the economic system should not intervene to protect savers who bought certain securities that then resulted in losses. It's the free market; it's fair to be that way. But is it really fair for it to be that way? Wasn't there a lack of information, a different market power? Then one can also say but if we protect savers from losses, at that point you don't stop, because then the people who had the Lehman Brothers securities, etc. should also be reimbursed. So deciding what is right to do becomes complicated, from what is we cannot derive what must be and every time we intervene we have to figure out by what criteria and where we stop.

What are the answers we have found? The first is the subjective type, we can call it "selfishness." Before utilitarianism comes selfishness, that is, the yardstick is me. It is a very simple rule, however, it does not work. For example I want to do anything to become rich and famous. Yes but rich and famous doesn't mean anything. If you are rich in the middle of the desert and you are starving, all the money is of no use to you. Being rich only serves you for other things, other goods/satisfactions you can get. Famous you could also be for a reason you are not happy to be or you are for very trivial things. As for the distinction between different forms of selfishness, in English there are two ways to define selfishness, egoist and selfish, which have slightly different meanings. Selfish is the slightly more animalistic one, that is, I want to come first and I don't give a damn about others. The slightly more evolved selfishness, in the sense of egoism, is that I am me and I decide what is important to me, which may be ensuring the best studies I can for my children. That's egoism but it's not that self-centeredness of someone who doesn't think about others, however, it's also not altruism because then I would have to pay for a stranger's studies. To understand this let's take the example of Hobbes' beggar. He was known to be an atheist and directed toward total utilitarianism, at one point it seems that someone saw him begging and accused him of not behaving in relation to his ideas. His response was that out of selfishness, he preferred to give them a coin to get them off his back. However, this theory has limitations because it can be shown that human nature is not always selfish; there are cases where there is real altruism. Like people who are tortured and despite the fact that the thing they most want and the thing that represents the most utility to them is for the torture to end, they don't talk. And so it is possible for one to do things out of stubbornness, because they think they are morally right, because they want to be choreographed/gentile, out of belonging (we saw with MacIntyre) etc. and not out of simple utility. There are logics of belonging that make it so that selfishness cannot be fully applied. One view of egoism is Nietzsche's view of the will to power. There are no rules, the famous phrase "god is dead," and the only rule that the true man, that is, the superman, follows is to assert himself. So utility is in the feeling of power, in doing what I want, while disutility is in anything that limits my will to power. Again, every once in a while in the news this thing a little bit leaks out, every once in a while there is some character who is a little bit over the top but sometimes he is justified because he is very good in his field, he is partly justified or anyway he thinks he is above convention because he is so good that he thinks he can do things a little bit out of the ordinary. For example, one may be Trump, who thinks he is the best of all, but he has made his fortune by ripping off his neighbor, not paying debts to banks, salaries, etc. Another one who has been tolerated for a long time is producer Weinstein, who used to take advantage a bit but because he was good, made everyone money, etc. he was tolerated. Someone who believes himself to be above good and evil, believes himself to be so good that he is above the conventions of ordinary mortals and very often these things are for a time tolerated precisely because of the advantages this person brings. It is a situation that can occur, and so Nietzsche's reasoning that seems to us a bit exaggerated now and then has some evidence, and it has it in the world of finance as well. You saw the Enron case for example, initially people like Fastow or Lay, they were maybe a little bit talked about, however, everybody followed them because they made money for everybody, lawyers, employees, shareholders. Maybe you wonder if it's all right what he's doing, however you consider this person a little bit beyond good and evil, so sometimes even in the world of finance this occurs, or rather, when there is a very powerful person the risk that a Nietzsche-like vision will be realized is always there. A very good one you tolerate a lot before you stop him, after that when things go wrong the patatrac happens but before that everything is fine. Another famous case we haven't seen is the Madoff case, who was for many years a highly respected person, embedded in the best circles. He only selected the best clientele, making them a lot of money, only they made their money with so-called Ponzi schemes, where the return on a certain investment is based on the payouts that come in, so if money keeps coming in there is no problem, you have the problem when people start asking you for reimbursement. At some point, you can't repay anymore and it all collapses. So rule breakers are there, it's Nietzsche-like selfishness, and they are put up with it at first. The last issue when it comes to utilitarianism is that you have to distinguish between desires and interests. This was the Bentham-Mill discourse if you remember. Desires, one says a pig who can eat whatever he wants is the ultimate in happiness, he has no thoughts, he eats like a pig and that is what interests him. Socrates on the other hand keeps thinking, his appetite goes away, he keeps having doubts, he never makes up his mind, and he spends his time striving. Mill said better Socrates unhappy than a happy pig, but if you measure enjoyment, maybe the pig on the scale of enjoyment is higher. Another argument of Mill was there are high pleasures and low pleasures, high pleasures are worth more. However, the objection to this is that is a Wagner concert better than a slice of bread and Nutella, but even so, a hundred slices of bread and Nutella don't add up to more than the Wagner concert? That is, there is such a number that by adding up so many low pleasures you arrive at the value of one high pleasure. From a logical point of view, there must be a certain amount of low pleasures that exceed a high pleasure, so the criticism to Mill remains this. What is the advantage of selfishness, which we have seen in the form of "hedonism" in the Cyrenaics? In ethical analysis it is a very easy key because anyone can identify that they like bread and Nutella better than stewed turnip, hard to find someone who says that unseasoned salad is tastier than dressed salad. So it is easy to understand hedonism, what pleasure is we know. In fact some people say it's very easy to know what pain is compared to pleasure, because pain is also often easy to locate, one says I have back pain and I would like to take a pill to make it go away. The feeling of well-being that one has from eating something is more diffuse, less localized because it is not in the stomach or mouth. This already is a difference that can be made between pain and pleasure, it is not exactly the opposite of pain. After that there is the argument that we have already seen in the transition from Cyrenaics to Epicureans, from Bentham to Mill. Also, pleasure sometimes is the result, for example, many of you will do some sports, even some strenuous sports like going to the mountains or going for a run and doing 1 hour of running, it's hard to say it's very pleasurable, you do it because you like having done it. Or playing some playstation game, it's the feeling of having succeeded that's the pleasure, not the thing itself. So it is not a localizable feeling to have won a game, but it is the result of a process, which is sometimes an unpleasant process as well. For example, if one runs at the limits of one's ability for a while one comes to feelings of unpleasantness, maybe he gets blisters on his feet. But if it was something too unpleasant he would not do it so the pleasure also as a result, and not as a sensation. This is what we have to say about hedonism and selfishness. After that, a completely different field concerning Aristotle, which also concerned Kant a little bit, is the so-called "virtue ethics." According to Aristotle there are some things that we do because we like them, but there are some things that we like because we believe they are right and we do them. Because we believe that playing golf is a good thing to do, when we have learned we take pleasure in it. One is motivated to learn something because he is interested in it, not because he liked it, because he doesn't know how to do it. After learning he is all happy and he likes it, however, the reasoning is backwards, that is, because it is an activity I value, I like it, but the pleasure comes after achieving it. So it is the famous concept of eudaimonia that we have seen, that is, well being rather than well-being. Aristotle's pleasure is not a nice cold beer when it is hot, that is well-being, but living well or well being. That is virtue ethics, that is the pleasure of doing things correctly. And as I said before, Aristotle makes this argument on the basis of that empirical observation that to us now doesn't come across so well, however he says there are activities that enhance that. If there is a plant and I water it, it grows. If I feed an animal, it grows. So I have to see what are the good things: those are the things that make me grow. A person grows when he studies, reasons, etc. much less when he drinks a beer. What makes you grow, what improves you is what is good for you, is the good. And so good according to Aristotle is acting according to virtue, the famous eudaimonia. Then unlike our thinking, he had a bit of an all-around reasoning, for example nowadays people excel in a few things, according to him the good life was one thing that led to excellence in so many fields, and actually he was a head case because he was a philosopher, physicist, mathematician, etc. a specialization in one thing according to Aristotle is not the excellence he has in mind. Excellence is a complete excellence. Then this thing here no longer works in a Darwinian world. Look at Aristotle's reasoning can be made very convincing, i.e. one can say it is true that one has to look at what makes one grow, water for a geranium is better than for a cactus, so what is good for a subject depends on the nature of that subject. Each subject has its own nature, and you have to follow its nature. This concept was later taken up by MacIntyre, namely the concept that there is a virtue ethic, so much so that his most famous book is called "after virtue." MacIntyre says we focus too much on too simple moral qualities like good/evil, but what accomplishes people's lives are richer qualities, which also contain in them recommendations. So if I say the cake is good, it doesn't mean it is good but it means I like it, it means I think it is nutritious so there is a judgment and together also a recommendation. If the cake is good, I eat it, if this thing is bad, I avoid it. So it's not good/bad and who cares, but good/bad and what I do next, that is, they also contain recommendations. Then we saw that good/bad does not solve the problem, because if I say hunting is good, it is good for the hunter but for the pheasant it is not. Another criticism that is made of this question of virtue is that many of these things are learned, i.e. if we want to criticize our world more we could say that good and evil is put into our heads by someone who is interested in controlling our behavior, which is not someone who is controlling us from afar but it is the whole of society, i.e. society agrees that people should work, that there should be a low rate of violence, etc. so one might imagine that we are in a giant zoo where we without realizing it are acting as trained animals, so virtue might be what masks the conditioning to which we are exposed. Since we have been exposed since before we were aware of it, we don't notice it. Look at this in itself, from a logical point of view it is not completely absurd. Harari's book that I recommended to you says that one of the explanations for the birth of agriculture, which is something from which there is no turning back, is that wheat colonized us, not vice versa, that is, one of the theories is that wheat grew in a certain area, in that area people gathered for religious reasons etc. and they found this plant that had a flavor that they liked. Wheat germinates very easily so people understand it. If one eats a cherry and spits out the stone, maybe after twenty years there is a cherry tree there but what does he know. If, on the other hand, wheat sprouts after a few months, he is quicker to understand that fact. So wheat, which was very suitable to be cultivated but requires a lot of care made man from a hunter to a farmer and therefore according to the provocative theory it is wheat that colonized us, not we who colonized wheat. In the sense that wheat needed someone to affirm it, and if you think about it it is like that for so many forms of life. So we participate in a society and we are conditioned, we are part of a pattern and we can no longer move away from it. Radical criticism of this, that is, the fact that we are part of a pattern and are conditioned by it, is "existentialism." Kierkegaard was a very complicated philosopher, inventor of existentialism, that is, how should I live? Good problem. Ethics is how I have to spend my life, and how I have to spend my life leads to anguish according to Kierkegaard, which he solved with aesthetic life, ethical life, religious life as forms of evolution, so aesthetic life with John always pursuing personal satisfactions but never getting away with it, ethical life with Abraham respecting God's will, and religious life which is really identified with doing God's will completely. Opposite but still on the same logic is Sartre: France, post-World War II, instead of being religious completely atheist.

Sartre's idea is that existence comes before essence, so asking why I exist, what is my nature, means nothing according to him. We don't even have to ask because human nature is to exist, existence comes before essence. So there is no divine design, there is no God, there is nothing, we just are. And criticizing Kierkegaard says let's test the case of Abraham who heard the voice of God, he must have wondered if it was the voice of God or if it was the voice of the devil? The moment he decides it is God's voice and agrees to sacrifice his son he has taken the responsibility, so his existence is the decisive part of the decision. So human beings according to Sartre are radically free, we cannot appeal to anything else and every action we take is our responsibility. This again is important because if you think about it it's also an argument that he makes, any decision maker, think of a

CEO, the moment he decides he is alone, he cannot rely on anything else. The only responsibility is his own, and this according to Sartre applies to any decision. So you can do and think all you want, but the moment you decide you cannot give responsibility to anyone else. From this comes anguish, which is the main feature, this in common with Kierkegaard, that is, the anguish of existing. And unlike Kierkegaard, since for Sartre God does not exist our existence is absurd, it leads nowhere, it means nothing but the fact that we exist, we come from nowhere, we go nowhere and we are forced to take responsibility without being able to invoke higher entities. When faced with a decision what can one do? Not choose, but according to Sartre not choosing is still a choice. Being distressed by a decision I stand still, but standing still is still a decision, so it's not that I get away with it, even inertia brings consequences, and since I pay the consequences, even inertia is a decision. The second way is good people, there is a source of value and I decide based on those values. The third way is people who behave well, take responsibility, but believing in something, some moral code, religious code, etc. According to Sartre, the mature position is one that somewhat resembles skepticism, I do things because I do them however without particularly believing in them. I do them as I think best but not because I think it is right to do them that way. The metaphor he uses is that of the waiter: each one of us at the later stage can imagine that he is a waiter, who follows certain rules, behaves in a certain way, however at any moment he could stop being a waiter and change completely, and he would have the same value. And we in our inner self know that. So one may decide to follow certain rules, to conform to the corporate culture etc. however, it is not that he is, he does. What he is is something else, so much so that according to Sartre he can decide at any time to change the way he behaves. So the only way for Sartre is authenticity, one must live by taking responsibility and without believing that he has the right answer. The classic example of authenticity he gives is that of the sincere Nazi. Many of us agree that Nazism was a rather significant evil. Those who adhered to Nazism could belong to different categories, there may be those who did it out of convenience, that is, imagine that there is a contest to be a professor and if there is a certain regime, whoever adheres more to the regime the more perhaps is advantaged in that contest, so out of convenience I profess to be a Nazi or belonging to certain political parties because it suits me. Then there may be those who did it out of obedience, if you are a public servant you either quit or you apply the laws that are there even if they are unjust. So one does it for career, the other one does it not to lose his career. After that, however, according to Sartre there could also be a quota, and there was, of sincere Nazis i.e., those who really thought that some rules invented by Nazism were just rules. They thought that the Aryan race was superior, that contamination should be avoided, etc. Hitler was a sincere Nazi for example. It seems that when the regime was now about to collapse he had said I may have done a lot of things wrong, but I was almost completing the project of eliminating the Jews. That is, he boasted that he had gone very far, that he had very little time left to finish this project. The sincere Nazi, as much as it bothers us to talk or think about it, lives in authenticity according to Sartre.

The Nazi returns with Kant. Kant's law of universalizability: to see if a rule is good you have to see if it is universalizable, and that is if it works if you extend it. So you can say, is telling lies right or wrong? If you universalize it you can't talk to anybody anymore, so society doesn't work anymore. Then what is universalizable can be turned into a categorical imperative. Let me remind you of the distinction between categorical imperative and hypothetical imperative. The hypothetical imperative is I do this thing because the categorical imperative is I just do this thing. Unfortunately, the law of the extermination of the Jews is universalizable and is a big critique of Kant. The sincere Nazi works in Kant's system, after all, Kant was also German. So unfortunately wrong rules can also be universalized. And this is a criticism that can be made of Kant's system. Another criticism that can be made of Kant's reasoning is that it only solves one part of the problem, this is there in Hume, and that is one thing is to figure out what to think, and another thing is to figure out what to do. For example, it is correct to study accounting because then the jobs that require knowing it are higher paying than others, so it is convenient for me. This seemingly innocent statement begs the question but will it be true? And so I go and look at the statistics regarding the fact that graduates in certain disciplines have higher salaries than others. But it doesn't actually tell us what to think, it tells us what to do. Because who said I have to wish to have a job where I get paid well? So practical reason is sometimes not enough. According to Hume, no desire is irrational, because no desire is contrary to reason, so we are conditioned by the correct desires i.e. I do a certain thing because then I accomplish another (hypothetical imperative). According to Hume, for example, it is not irrational that I would rather all mankind die than get a scratch. This may not be practical reasoning, but from the theoretical point of view, it is not illogical. From the rational point of view if each person thinks only of his own desires I can invent any scale of values, so even some of Kant's reasoning can be discussed.

In "utilitarianism," the most important thing is utilitarianism of acts and utilitarianism of rules. The utilitarianism of acts does not like it because it is the one that says take a bum and take away his organs because you have to give them to five people who maybe will make important scientific discoveries but you can't use another one, even though from a point of view of calculating utility it might fit. This is called act utilitarianism, you can do an accounting of the utility of individual people, and you can do an accounting of happiness. Better is the utilitarianism of rules, that is, what signals I send if I do something like this, it's convenient to behave this way, how society interprets it, and so it looks at the remote aspects. Rule utilitarianism looks precisely at the remote consequences, looking at the remote consequences can be useful but is a bit illusory, the remote consequences are all the consequences. This gives rise to the example of the literary character of Don Quixote, that is, a subject with a very strong moral code who devotes his life to a chivalric code that no one gives a damn about. According to Kant this subject works very well. In the utilitarian world he is a moron, because he wastes his life and wastes other people's time on things that do not exist, that are outdated. So he puts his all into it, great enthusiasm, high ideals, etc., but the battle is useless and unrealistic, it is useless. According to Kant he would be a positive character because he follows his ideal, the behavior cannot be very generalized but the ideal of adhering to a chivalrous code can. The problem is that you say let's evaluate the consequences, if we think about the consequences, when do you stop with the consequences? For example take the famous case of the outbreak of World War I. Gavrilo Princip shoots the archduke heir to the throne of Austria-Hungary and war breaks out (Sarajevo bombing). The anecdote says that this bombing happened by accident because the driver of the imperial motorcade took a wrong turn and went into a dead end, the escort could not intervene, shots were fired, and then everything happened.

Before World War I, the situation in Europe was very prosperous. If you read the book "Yesterday's World" by Zweig, in this book he tells about the situation of Europe before World War I and they were fine, they were traveling, there was peace, the last war had been in 1870, it seemed that wars were no more. Later with World War I, a crazy mess happened that lasted maybe until 1989. Was it the driver's fault? That is, when do we stop with the consequences? Then especially if one says it's the driver's fault, the driver might say but it's the fault of the one who had not given me the right instructions, it's the fault of the one who chose that soldier to be the driver, so his commander, and you never end. What are the consequences to be evaluated in a utilitarian calculation? You distinguish between consequences that could have been foreseen, so if you put someone without a license driving the emperor's car and he crashes into a tree, that could have been foreseen. If, on the other hand, a good driver drives the car but by chance he makes a wrong turn and then everything else, it can't be his fault because those consequences could not have been foreseen, so in the utilitarian calculation you should put only the consequences you could have foreseen. So at the time, you decide you have to evaluate the foreseeable consequences, after the action you have to evaluate the actual consequences. And here again, there is a criticism of Kant, he says what matters is motive, so if I don't cheat on exams because then who knows what people think of me, wrong. I must not copy on exams because on exams you don't copy, that is the categorical imperative. So according to Kant, you have to do what is right and not what is convenient for you. But in terms of consequences this has been challenged because one says okay, and then let's imagine the case where one wants to do good, so one buys some drugs and sends them to an African country where there is some major health problem. Chance would have it that because of a storage defect or for some reason beyond his control that drug instead of saving lives, it degrades and kills people. Should we hold him responsible? He had the best intentions but he produces a very negative effect. So without medication, 10% die, and with the wrong medication 50% die. Is he responsible? We could say no if he had done all the preventive works, etc. Let's take the opposite case.

A bandit hates his neighbor and tries to run him over with his car however the neighbor notices, tries to move, and in moving avoids a flower pot or tree falling on his head that would have killed him. And so not only does he not run him over, he saves him because if he had done nothing, a flowerpot would have fallen on his head and he would have died. Should we thank the neighbor just because the result is good? Does the motivation or the result matter? Sometimes there are different consequences than anticipated consequences, so you have to look at both, the actual consequences and the anticipated consequences, you have to consider the motive, but you cannot be kept exempt from the consequences. Then there is one last thing about utility, which is related to how you measure happiness: you cannot measure it. And then does total happiness count or does average happiness count? If total happiness counted, that is, if you could do an accounting of happiness between those who have the advantages and those who have the disadvantages, you could add them up. But imagine that a person should be born or be admitted into a certain community a person who is less happy than the average of those who are already in that community. In terms of total happiness, this increases because if you take nothing away from those who were already there and add one even who is not very well off however who is not completely unhappy, total happiness increases. The average happiness decreases, but if you look at this you never end because if you want to produce an increase in average happiness you kill them all until only the happiest one is left. That's not good, so pay attention to happiness accounting as well.

The last idea we focused on is "contractualism." People can decide to come to an agreement. If I agree with a person or was otherwise present at the decision, if I agreed or did nothing to disassociate myself, that means I was okay with it. In the social contract this question is not there. Talking about Locke we saw tacit consent, and let's also recover another philosopher we talked about who is Hume. Hume's state of nature is one in which because people according to him are selfish, you live badly, everyone goes around with a knife between their teeth because they are afraid someone else will attack them. This is the lawless state of nature.

In a Nietzsche world this particular thing doesn't suit the weak, the world of crime for example works a little bit like that, there are no laws and so you can never be safe because as soon as you lose a little bit of strength you get taken out. And so the state of nature is very tiring, that's why you make a social contract, you agree to abide by certain rules so that you can live a little bit more peacefully outside the state of nature. According to Locke this agreement is tacit and can be assumed. None of us has ever been asked if we are okay with living in this economic system, political system, etc., and except for a few cases of people who reject convention (so rare that they make movies about it like "in to the wild") you are embedded in a system of social conventions that you did not choose. According to Locke you gave tacit consent, according to others it is not at all true that you gave tacit consent because no one asked you to and therefore you could not say no but I would prefer the society where there was slavery or I would prefer another historical period. The only thing you can do is drop out and leave but that is something that occurs very rarely. Rawls solves this with the veil of ignorance, consent is not tacit but presumed, that is, if you were to express your consent now, would you give it? And to which system would you give it? The main criticism of Rawls' thought of the veil of ignorance is that it may apply in comparative terms, not in absolute terms. In comparative terms it means: let's imagine that I see badly, I have this handicap. If one has the handicap that he sees badly what is the society that helps him the most? Maybe the one where there is voice description of commands, etc. So put that is fine, but we have to make a law where there is for certain things voice description of commands or if I have a hard time walking that there be access ramps, that there be handicap parking, etc. They cost money, however, not knowing where you will be, behind the veil of ignorance would you rather bear small costs so that a few people have a better life or not? So if you compare two comparative situations the discourse of the veil of ignorance works quite a bit, it doesn't work in absolute terms, i.e. to say this system is good because it would be the one I would choose not comparatively to another but in absolute terms, I don't know, because I am conditioned by what I know. So it is criticized from this point of view.

Last idea that comes from contractualism and is not controversial is the idea that there are rules that we are comfortable with but we are also comfortable that there is someone who forces us to abide by them and punishes us if we do not abide by them. For example, we are fishermen on a lake and we know that if each of us catches 10 kilograms of fish a day, the fish has time to reproduce, etc. if each of us catches too much then the fish will not reproduce and next year we will all starve. In game theory what happens? The rational equilibrium would be that we agree and each one gets his 10 kilograms of fish by fishing for one hour a day. But immediately one realizes that if he fishes 3 hours a day instead of 10 kilos he catches 30 kilos, and the part he doesn't eat he sells by taking a lot of money. Since it doesn't take a genius to think of this, everyone does it right away despite the fact that everyone agrees that it would be more rational for the overall output to fish only one hour because if the fish reproduces in one year it grows 100 tons of fish, if I catch it all right away it grows only one ton. However, for each person it is rational to be smart. Unless there is the famous social contract in which we elect a political entity that forces us all to abide by those rules and punishes us if we do not abide by them.

At that point we would be happy to abide by the rules because we are sure that others abide by them as well and no one fishes more than we do. This by the way also explains the degeneration of social systems when there is not enough political strength and someone who is credible to enforce the rules. It is the famous theory of the "broken window" i.e. as long as something is intact no one touches it, when it starts to break then it degenerates very quickly. So Rawls' social contract but also a collective choice that binds us all and that we are all obliged to respect. An example as far as the financial world is concerned is insider trading, that is, if I have good news I would be smart. If everyone who has the good news is being smart, people in the market take shenanigans and no longer go to the market, so even those who lived in the market lose the ability to continue trading in the market because they are not credible. But no one alone has the incentive to behave well even knowing that otherwise this thing happens. So we need an authority to compel and fine us if we don't do this to give confidence in the market, confidence that everyone needs. The same thing applies to financial statement disclosure, you know that companies are a complicated reality, and every now and then unforeseen things happen, so the first impulse that comes to a certain person is to say ok, I don't write it like this now, next year I will fix it. But if you lose credibility in accounting/financial reporting the whole information loses so it suits everybody to that we have rules and sanctions that force compliance.

Thank you for getting to the end of the book, I have spent a lot of time writing the manuscript and I ask you to help me with the dissemination of the book. It would be very helpful

if you would leave me a positive review on AMAZON. Thank you very much!

Thank you!!!!!

Bibliography

1. Alemanni B., Behavioral finance: discovering the mistakes that make us lose money, 2015

2. Barber & Odean, The Courage of Mis guided Convictions. Financial Analysts Journal, p.47, 1999

3. Barontini R., "Finance for International Innovation Handout," typescript, 2015

4. Beyond Greed and Fear: Understanding Behavioral Finance and the Psychology of Investing, shefrin,2002

5. Bolognesi E., Tasca R., "The role of the benchmark between past and future," 2009

6. Burton E., Edwin, and Sunit Shah, Behavioral Finance : Understanding the Social, Cognitive, and Economic Debates, Jonh Wiley & Sons, incorporated, 2013

7. Cervellati E. M. , "Behavioral finance and investment," Mc Graw-Hill, Milan, 2012.

8. De Marchi Gianluigi, "Choosing the right fund: how to use the benchmark to Evaluating asset management products," 2001

9. Fischhoff and Beyth "I know it would happen"- remembered probabilities of once future things pp. 1-16 1975

10. Survey of Italians' Savings and Financial Choices, Intesa San paolo 2017

11. Survey on Savings and Financial Choices of Italians,Intesa San paolo 2018

12. Izzo C., Financial investments, the instruments, products, processes, and services. Characteristics and evaluation criteria, Sole 24ore Group, 2007

13. Jones B. "Bounded Rationality" Annual Riview political science, 1999, pg 297-321

14. Legrenzi P., Psychology and financial investment, Il Sole 24 Ore ,2006

15. Investment choices of Italian households Consob report, 2019

16. Levy, J. S. (1992), An Introduction to Prospect Theory. PoliticalPsychology, 13(2), pp. 171-186.

17. Liera M., The Common Funds, Il Sole 24 Ore, 2005.

18. Linciano N., Cognitive errors and preference instability in the investment choices of Retail savers, Consob, January 2010

19. Lo Conte M., The words of savings: overconfidence, IL Sole 24Ore, April 22, 2017

20. Lopes L., Between Hope and Fear: The Psychology Of Risk, In Advances In. Experimental Social Psychology, 20, 255-295, 1987

21. Lusardi A., Mitchell O. S. , The economic importance of financial literacy: theory and evidence 2008, Journal of economic literature, 2014

22. Matloff, Roger, Chaillou, Joy Hunter, Nonprofit_Investment_and_Development_Solutions, a guide to thriving

in today's economy, john wiley & sons, incorporated, 2013

23. McNeil BJ, Pauker SG, Sox HC, Tversky A. On the elicitation of preferences for alternative therapies. New England Journal of Medicine 1982; 21: 1259-62.

24. Miller G. A., The magical number seven, plus or minus two: some limits on our capacity for processing information, 1956

25. Proto A., The business of banks: operations and services, Giappichelli editore, 2018

26. Ricciardi V., Simon H. K., What is behavioral finance?, Business education and technology journal, Fall 2002

27. Rigoni U., Behavioral finance and asset management, G. GiappichelliEditor,Turin,2006

28. Samuelson W., Zeckhauser R., Status quo bias in decision making. Journal of Risk and Uncertainty, 1, pp. 7-59, 1988.

29. Shefrin H., Beyond Greed and Fear: Understanding Behavioral Finance and the Psychology of Investing, 1999

30. Tversky A, Kahneman D., Judgment under Uncertainty: Heuristics and Biases, science, new series, 1974

31. Tversky A., Kahneman D., Prospect Theory: An Analysis of Decision under Risk. Author(s): Source: Econometrica, Vol. 47, No. 2 Mar. , 1979, pp. 263-292

32. Tversky A, Kahneman D. The framing of decisions and psychology of choice. Science; 211: 453-458, 1981.

33. Tversky A, Kahneman D., Extensional Versus Intuitive Reasoning: The Conjunction. Fallacy in Probability Judgment, 1983

34. Tversky, A. and D. Kahneman, Advances in Prospect Theory: Cumulative Representation of Uncertainty, Journal of Risk and Uncertainty, 5, pp. 297-323, 1992

35. Tversky A., Kahneman D. Choices, values and frames, 2000.

36. Weinstein & Klein, 1996, cited in Puri & Robinson, Optimism and economic choice. Journal of Financial Economics, p.76, 2006

Made in the USA
Las Vegas, NV
15 May 2024

89980382R00148